Help–

My Kid Is Driving Me Crazy

Help–
My Kid Is Driving Me Crazy

**The 17 Ways Kids
Manipulate Their Parents,
and What You Can Do About It**

DAVID SWANSON, Psy.D.

A Perigee Book

A PERIGEE BOOK
Published by the Penguin Group
Penguin Group (USA) Inc.
375 Hudson Street, New York, New York 10014, USA
Penguin Group (Canada), 90 Eglinton Avenue East, Suite 700, Toronto, Ontario M4P 2Y3, Canada
(a division of Pearson Penguin Canada Inc.) • Penguin Books Ltd., 80 Strand, London WC2R
0RL, England • Penguin Group Ireland, 25 St. Stephen's Green, Dublin 2, Ireland (a division
of Penguin Books Ltd.) • Penguin Group (Australia), 250 Camberwell Road, Camberwell,
Victoria 3124, Australia (a division of Pearson Australia Group Pty. Ltd.) • Penguin Books
India Pvt. Ltd., 11 Community Centre, Panchsheel Park, New Delhi—110 017, India
• Penguin Group (NZ), 67 Apollo Drive, Rosedale, North Shore 0632, New Zealand
(a division of Pearson New Zealand Ltd.) • Penguin Books (South Africa) (Pty.) Ltd.,
24 Sturdee Avenue, Rosebank, Johannesburg 2196, South Africa

Penguin Books Ltd., Registered Offices: 80 Strand, London WC2R 0RL, England

While the author has made every effort to provide accurate telephone numbers and Internet
addresses at the time of publication, neither the publisher nor the author assumes any responsibility for errors, or for changes that occur after publication. Further, the publisher does not
have any control over and does not assume any responsibility for author or third-party websites
or their content.

First edition: September 2009

Perigee trade paperback ISBN: 978-0-399-53526-0

Library of Congress Cataloging-in-Publication Data

Swanson, David, 1969–
    Help—my kid is driving me crazy : the 17 ways kids manipulate their parents, and
what you can do about it / David Swanson.
        p. cm.
    Includes index.
    ISBN 978-0-399-53526-0   4236 8257 '/10
    1. Parent and child. 2. Parenting. 3. Child rearing. 4. Manipulative behavior in
children. 5. Communication in the family. I. Title.
    HQ755.85.S917 2009
    649'.1—dc22   2009018903

PRINTED IN THE UNITED STATES OF AMERICA

10 9 8 7 6 5 4 3 2 1

Most Perigee books are available at special quantity discounts for bulk purchases for sales pro-
motions, premiums, fund-raising, or educational use. Special books, or book excerpts, can also
be created to fit specific needs. For details, write: Special Markets, Penguin Group (USA) Inc.,
375 Hudson Street, New York, New York 10014.

To William, Nicolas, and Andrew

I will never be perfect, but know that
I am committed to being the best dad I can be.

CONTENTS

The 17 Ways Kids Manipulate Their Parents

Children demand instant gratification, and toward that end they use tools that they acquire through trial and error to satisfy short-term goals. They use these tools because they work; by understanding them and you can learn how to avoid being manipulated. The long-term goals are better parenting and a happier family life.

Emotional Blackmail: "I'll stay sad until he gives me what I want." (Page 27)

Punishment: "If I can't get what I want, at least I can get even." (Page 32)

Shutting Down: "I can't hear a word you're saying." (Page 40)

Irrational Logic: "Why can't I stay out all night? It's not like I'm doing drugs." (Page 46)

Negotiation: "Let me go just this once, and I promise I'll do all my homework." (Page 52)

Confrontation and Protest: "If asking doesn't work, I'll throw a tantrum." (Page 57)

Steamrolling: "Can I? Can I? Can I?" ... "How about now?" (Page 67)

Covert Operations: "Face it—being a kid means you sometimes lie, deceive, withhold." (Page 74)

Divide and Conquer: "But Dad said . . ." "But Mom said . . ." (Page 82)

Tactical Engagement: "If I can keep them talking about it, maybe they'll give in." (Page 88)

Creating Leverage: "I did everything you said today, so I should be able to . . ." (Page 97)

Playing the Victim: "I'm the *only* one in the house who never gets to." (Page 101)

Forging the Friendship: "But gee, Dad, aren't we pals after all?" (Page 105)

Character Comparison: "Susie's parents are cool. What's wrong with you?" (Page 112)

Casting Doubt: "I'll get beat up." "I won't pass the class if you don't let me." (Page 117)

Glorification: "This is the only chance I'll every have to do this." (Page 123)

Surprise Attack: "When all else fails, catch Mom off guard." (Page 128)

Introduction

As a parent, you have likely noticed that there are many well-written parenting guides that typically go into great detail about how to set limits for your child to make for a more harmonious family environment. There are also parenting experts who will tell you how to get your child to follow directions and to behave. These books and experts tell you a lot about the *mechanics* of good parenting, and often a light of recognition is turned on. But something is missing. You try to apply what you read and you still find that your child does not respond or responds temporarily before going his own way.

In a favorite catchphrase, most experts will tell you that your child doesn't follow directions because "you have failed to be consistent," and that you have failed to be consistent because you have not applied a consequence every time your child engages in inappropriate behavior. In retrospect, you recognize this failure on your part, but why have you failed? You want to do the right thing, but you don't follow through. Why do you have such a difficult time remaining consistent with your child? After all, you have been told either by books or by professionals that your child will respond only if you, the parent, are consistent in delivering consequences. If you are inconsistent, you shoot yourself in the foot.

Are you really a glutton for punishment? Are you addicted to fighting endlessly with your daughter to pick up after herself? to wake up on time? to do her homework? Of course not. Perhaps you are unable to be consistent because of a dynamic that exists within your interaction with her. Imagine this: While you are worrying over your own consistency, your child is doing everything within her power to ensure that you are not consistent. And why would she do this? The following pages will share insights I have gathered over years of clinical practice that may help you reexamine your beliefs.

As a psychologist who has worked with thousands of families in conflict, I have found that parents are often puzzled about why their children act the way they do. Every day in my office, parents utter the same pleas for help: "We don't understand why he always has to fight with us!" or "We need help! Getting her to respond is a constant battle." (Since all the issues in this book pertain to parents and children of both sexes, I will vary third-person singular pronouns when used in a generic sense.) Keep in mind that these parents may have read the books that you have read. They have been told exactly how to reward their child's positive responses. And they have been taught how to deliver an appropriate consequence when their child has failed to respond. These parents are not uninformed. Nor are they bad parents. They are good parents, just like you and me, but they are frustrated. And they are frustrated because they cannot figure out how to get their child to follow directions and behave.

As a parent and a psychologist, I have spent a great deal of time observing the interactions of children and parents in an effort to identify why parents struggle with their children's behavior. I have examined my relationship with my own children. I have also taken time to reflect on my childhood and the misery I inflicted on my parents. They deserve an award for the fact that I am still around to write this book. I wanted to better understand why children don't respond (or respond negatively) to their parents' wishes. My observations have led me to a new perspective on why children are defiant and fail to follow directions. This perspective brought me to new ideas that I believe will revolutionize the way you parent your child.

I have come to the conclusion that children rely on seventeen unique ways to manipulate their parents in order to get what they want. I call these seventeen manipulation strategies the *Tools of Power.*

This book will serve as a manual to guide you through the obstacle course of your child's seventeen Tools of Power. It will help you understand why your child manipulates and will give you the countertools to respond effectively. It will also help you understand why you, as a parent, fall prey to your child's Tools of Power, and it will enable you to decrease his need to use them in the future.

Most parents know some basic mechanics of parenting. They punish their child for inappropriate forms of behavior, and they may reward their child for appropriate behavior. These parents have learned that negative behavior decreases if it is met with punishment and that appropriate behavior increases with rewards. I refer to the methods of punishment and reward as the *mechanics* of parenting.

If you have purchased this book, you are probably not happy with your degree of success using the mechanics of parenting. Don't feel alone. Many parents feel frustrated because they find that the mechanics of parenting do not always work. The mechanics of parenting sometimes fail, but not because they are faulty. Punishment really does decrease inappropriate behavior, and happily, rewards increase appropriate behavior. The mechanics of parenting fail because of an emotional process that takes place during your attempt to employ them. More specifically, punishments and rewards fail because your child has figured out how to push your emotional buttons so that you become inconsistent. He pushes your emotional buttons through the use of his Tools of Power.

Every parent has emotional buttons—that is, the triggers to our most sensitive responses. The primary purpose for a child's use of a Tool of Power is to push emotional buttons to get what she wants or to even the score. For example, you may find it difficult to accept your child's expression of sadness. If so, your child can push your emotional buttons simply by crying. Perhaps you have a strong need for your child to show you respect. If so, your child can push your emotional buttons by treating you disrespectfully. As a reaction to emotional button pushing, you may be left feeling anxious, angry, or sad. Either way, if your child pushes your emotional buttons, she does it to be gratified. Your child is gratified by your reaction to her emotional button pushing. Emotional button pushing often goes something like this: The child's anger compels her to want to even the score and make her parent angry as well. Further, she instinctively knows that she can upset her parent by continuing to ask for what she wants; it has worked before. A typical scenario goes like this:

CHILD: I want a cookie.

PARENT: Not now. We're about to eat dinner.

CHILD (whining): But, Mom, I'll eat dinner. Can I have just one cookie?

PARENT (firmly): No. Not until after dinner.

CHILD (realizing she won't get the cookie, she becomes angry): I hate that rule. I want a cookie now!

PARENT (tension in voice): Ask me again and you won't get one after dinner.

CHILD: How about half now and half later?

PARENT (yelling): I said no! No means no!

CHILD (playing into Mom's anger): Well, you don't have to yell about it. I just asked for a cookie.

In this case, the parent falls prey to the child's emotional button pushing and is exploited by a Tool of Power that I call Punishment. Her angry emotional reaction has gratified the child. Mom's anger is precisely the reaction her daughter needs in order to know that her Tool of Power has been effective. In this case, the child's defiant behavior is rewarded. And this parent will have to contend with similar forms of behavior in the future because, for the child, the tool has worked: It has proven to be an effective way to alleviate her intense feelings of anger.

Emotional button pushing is very powerful. Most children

report that using a Tool of Power is so gratifying that the satisfaction they derive from pushing those buttons surpasses any fear they have of consequences. It is safe to say that if your child were to be placed in a position in which she felt compelled to push your emotional buttons, all the while knowing that she would be punished for doing so, she would go ahead and do it anyway. Seeing your reaction to her button pushing is that gratifying. And this is precisely the reason that the mechanics of parenting fail.

Parents who fall prey to emotional button pushing do so because they mistakenly believe that the mechanics of parenting always work and that children can maintain a mature degree of empathy when they are emotionally invested in getting what they want. It also assumes that children are capable of delaying gratification. These are three common misconceptions that you need to understand and overcome to avoid falling prey to frustration.

What follows will enable you to understand these common misconceptions and will lead you to the primary purpose of this book: to educate you on the seventeen ways your child manipulates, and to teach you to avoid being manipulated. I call these seventeen manipulation strategies Tools of Power because they are the only real power your child possesses in his relationship with you. And they are quite powerful indeed because they draw on your vulnerabilities as a parent. These seventeen Tools of Power work because your child has figured out how to successfully push your emotional buttons to get what he wants.

Don't be overly alarmed if your child exhibits the behaviors described in this book. Manipulative behavior is not an indication that your child is lacking moral character. It doesn't mean he is a terrible person. It mostly means he has not reached the level of maturity to be able to delay gratification. It also means that he has certain needs that he wants met. His manipulative behavior is his way of getting those needs met.

But as a parent, your main goal isn't getting his needs met. Your goal is nurturing, protecting, and strengthening your child so he can learn to operate in the world successfully. And success isn't measured by always getting your own way. Children who master the Tools of Power, thereby manipulating their parents to satisfy their amorphous instant gratification, don't usually become successful adults. They become narcissists with lifelong relationship problems.

So your goal is to nullify those Tools of Power—render them ineffective.

In the last part of this book, I am going to share with you a method I have developed that will help you assess your child's temperament. Although many of your child's needs appear to be immediate, such as wanting a cookie or a toy, there is always an underlying need that's not being met. I believe that you will be able to reduce the frequency of your child's manipulation in the future by developing a home structure specifically designed to meet the needs of his temperament.

But first, I want you to understand and know how to identify the Tools of Power your child uses to get his way with you. Once you become aware of these tools, you will be better able to protect yourself against them, and you will find yourself on the road to more successful parenting. And that is the goal of this book. But beware: Most children have more than one tool in their repertoire, and they may try more than one at a time, or quickly switch from one that isn't working to another one that may get the job done. One of the goals of this book is to acquaint you with all these variations and equip you to counteract them.

Each of the seventeen tools is followed by a countermeasure that I have found effective in my practice. After all, what good is recognition without the key to a solution?

Here are the keys. Don't ever forget: You are in the driver's seat.

PART ONE

HOW DID WE GET HERE?

The Truth About Kids, Parents,
and the Unspoken Dynamics Between Them

The Three Major Misconceptions Most Parents Believe

Before we discuss the various ways that children manipulate, we need to discuss three common misconceptions that many parents believe:

1. The mechanics of parenting always work.

2. Your child possesses empathy when she is emotionally invested in getting what she wants.

3. Your child possesses a strong ability to delay gratification.

You will be happier and more successful after you let go of these illusions. Hold on to them, and you will remain frustrated and ineffectual. Don't let parenting descend to an emotional battle. Effective parenting is only sabotaged by your emotional reactions. As stated in the introduction, it is your emotional reaction that typically gratifies your child but leads to a breakdown in the mechanics of parenting. Your child will gladly accept a consequence if it means that he'll get to push your emotional buttons and see you react in return. The gratification derived from gaining control over a parent's emotional reactions outweighs any fear of consequences.

Let's discuss these three misconceptions and work toward developing a more realistic perspective on the dynamics of parenting to reduce the risk of frustration.

FIRST MISCONCEPTION
The Mechanics of Parenting Always Work

Before you can understand why your child manipulates, you need to fully appreciate that *your child does what he does because it works*. It is only after you understand and accept this fact that you will truly understand how your child's misbehavior works for him. When I make this assertion in my private practice, many parents are confused. They say that it is impossible for their child to benefit from defiant behavior when that defiance is met with punishment. Although I understand the logic behind this, I insist that this way of thinking is wrong.

First of all, this way of thinking assumes the perspective of the parent. Your child views the world from an entirely different perspective. Most adults tend to be logical and approach problems or situations by considering future consequences. Fully functional adults place a higher value on decisions reached through logic rather than those reached through emotion. But a child typically reacts from his emotions rather than from logic. And when he is emotionally invested in getting his way, he doesn't consider future consequences—only what he wants at the moment. An example of this process is when your child responds to your threat of punishment by saying, "I don't care what you do." Your child would not say this if he feared he had more to lose by doing so. He is reacting to the emotion he feels, which in this case may be anger. Statements like this work for your child when he is angry. Such a statement allows him to act out his anger in a way that is cathartic. By making this type of statement, he is able to relieve much of the tension derived from anger. This is one way that defiant behavior can work for your child, and if a parent becomes frustrated in response to such an action, it is not only causing the mechanics of parenting to fail but also bringing gratification to the child. An angry child wants to see his parent equally upset as well.

The second reason the mechanics of parenting do not always work is that they are based entirely on the delivery of a reward or a punishment in response to a child's behavior. Punishments are exacted to discourage a particular behavior, while a reward is given to encourage a behavior. It sounds simple, but there are other things at play when you are parenting your child. *Most of what drives your child's behavior is emotion.* Think about it. Most parenting problems occur when your child is exhibiting an emotional response. When your child is emotionally invested in getting what he wants, he will attempt to push your buttons in the way that benefits him most. Although your child's Tools of Power come in seventeen forms, the success of any form of manipulation depends on your child's ability to push your emotional buttons. If you fall prey to this emotional current and rely only on the mechanics of parenting, you stand a greater chance of being ineffective with your child.

The impact of our emotions on parenting is enormous. Parents cannot remain consistent with their children when they are emotionally reactive. Any emotional reaction on your part not only interferes with your ability to remain consistent but also serves as gratification for your child in that he has gained the power to get a specific reaction out of you. When you display the emotional response he is after, you are providing the positive feedback he needs to know that he has succeeded in manipulating you.

It is impossible for any parent to be consistent 100 percent of the time, but consistency is worth striving for. If you can accurately understand the perspective of your child and how his defiance works for him, you will gain an advantage that will help you remain calm and consistent. This is what separates this book from other books on the market. To simply focus on the mechanics of parenting is not enough. You need to be aware of your emotional responses and the ways they gratify your child. It is this gratification that leads your child to use his Tools of Power.

Simply put, the Tools of Power allow your child to push your emotional buttons in the way that serves him best. Button pushing is your child's way of satisfying his wants without suffering consequences or punishment. Button pushing can be used to punish you, the parent, when you do not give your child what he wants, or may be used to gain your love, attention, and nurturance when he wishes to feel closer. Regardless of the purpose, you must understand that the Tools of Power are designed to work beneath the mechanical level of parenting. They are much more complex. The Tools of Power attack the underlying emotions that exist in every aspect of parenting. If you rely only on the mechanics of parenting and ignore the emotional button pushing on the part of your child, you will always be frustrated because the mechanics of parenting are sabotaged by emotions, which are much more powerful.

SECOND MISCONCEPTION
Your Child Possesses Empathy When She Is Emotionally Invested in Getting What She Wants

In my private practice, I meet with many parents who are anguished over their child's seeming lack of empathy. These parents complain, "I don't think she really cares about me, because if she did, she wouldn't hurt my feelings by lying to me," or "How could she say such hurtful things to me? Doesn't she know how badly it hurts my feelings?" My answer to that question is yes. But I would caution: Don't personalize what isn't personal.

Every child lies. And though it may seem hard to believe, if your child lies to you, she is not thinking about how it will hurt you. Lying is a strategy. When your child lies, she is only thinking of the best way either to avoid a consequence or to get what she wants. Don't think of lying as a personal attack.

The same is true for hurtful words and actions. As painful as they may be, the child's words and actions do not mean that she doesn't care about you. Your child is only using the strategy of exploiting your emotional vulnerability in order to get what she wants. Unfortunately, when your child is focused on getting what she wants, she is not concerned with your feelings. This is why I often tell parents to avoid personalizing their children's painful words or behavior. Hurtful or malicious statements may be an attempt by your child to punish you for an injustice she feels you delivered to her, or they may represent an attempt to cause you so much grief or frustration that you will eventually give in to her demands.

Many parents feel that their child should be more compassionate and empathetic. If you are a parent who feels this way, realize this: When your child is emotionally invested in getting her way, she has no empathy. And to go even further, let me also say that this lack of empathy is developmentally normal until midway through your child's later teenage years. This idea is a very provocative one. However, nothing could be closer to the truth. You need to understand that your child is still in the process of maturing. And from an early age, until later in adolescence, her inability to delay gratification and her strong desire to get what she wants far outweigh consideration for the feelings of others. The only exception is when exploiting the feelings of others around her will improve her chances of getting what she wants. Understanding your child's lack of empathy when she is emotionally invested in getting what she wants will save you a lot of frustration and pain.

In order to avoid falling prey to much of your child's emotional button pushing, you must always keep in mind that when your child is invested in getting her way, she sees you as having no feelings. You are only an object that gets her what she wants or prevents her from getting what she wants. I use the word "object" because objects are devoid of feelings. If you are the object that gets your child what she wants, she will attempt to manipulate you in order to get it. If you are the object that stands in the way of her getting what she wants, she will do her best to move you out of the way. Your feelings aren't her primary concern, but they may very well serve as a means to push your emotional buttons in order to improve her chances of getting what she wants.

Please understand that I am not suggesting that your child is totally incapable of being empathetic. She lacks empathy only when she is emotionally invested in getting what she wants. At other times, she is probably very compassionate. I have yet to meet a child who wasn't kind at heart.

THIRD MISCONCEPTION
Your Child Possesses a Strong Ability to Delay Gratification

Your child does not manipulate because he is lacking moral character. For the most part, your child probably tries very hard to please those around him. Your child will usually manipulate because his coping skills are not yet developed enough to contain the impulsive urges and anxiety he feels when he is blocked from getting something he badly wants or when he must experience something he wishes to avoid. You need to understand this before you can intervene effectively with your child. If you only parent from the adult perspective, you will personalize his behavior and be perpetually challenged to stay calm and remain objective. To be an effective parent, you need to understand that your child lacks the mature coping skills needed to delay gratification.

I refer to the child's approach in getting what he wants as the "I-WIN" mentality. "I-WIN" stands for "I Want It Now." On the other hand, adults operate from the "TOE" mentality. Adults like to stay well grounded in their approach to the world and value "Thoughts Over Emotion" when pursuing their goals. Adults possess a stronger ability to delay gratification. The mechanics of parenting draw from the adult perspective and the mistaken assumption that a child is able to plan ahead and to delay gratification. But this is misguided because it is based in the belief that your child will alter his behavior in consideration of future consequences. If you make this assumption, you will wind up frustrated, because a child usually lacks these attributes. This is particularly true when he is emotionally invested in getting his way. When your child knows what he wants, he will approach it from an I-WIN mentality. He will not want to delay his gratification, and depending on how badly he wants something, he may do everything within his power to get it. Logical rationales may make sense to you, but your child is unable to contain the anxiety of anticipation. As a result, your child may have great difficulty in removing himself from the present moment in order to understand how an immediate behavior may affect his future or bring about punishment.

As your child matures, so does his ability to delay gratification. This happens because his ability to cope with anticipation and the anxiety of having to wait improves. In addition, your child gains impulse control, which allows him to begin to think before he acts. As your child gradually matures, he begins to leave behind his I-WIN tendencies and starts to operate from the TOE mode.

These modes of thinking become clearer when we apply them to a life situation, such as Christmas morning. Your child, who normally fights to the death to avoid getting out of bed to go to school, is suddenly up at 5:00 a.m. He makes as much noise as possible and perhaps even goes to the extreme of jumping on your bed as you attempt to sneak in a few more minutes of sleep. He wants you to rise and shine, too, so that he can see what Santa has brought him. He just can't wait. *But you can*. Now, before you answer by saying, "Santa didn't bring any gifts for you," I urge you to think about the feeling you get in response to seeing the joy in your child's face as he tears into those gifts. *You do have something to gain*. But unlike him, you can cope with the anxiety of anticipation. You know that whether it is 5:00 a.m. or 10:00 a.m., you will still feel that joy. Your child's I-WIN perspective does not lead to the same conclusion because, for him, it has to be done NOW!

As your child matures, he will begin to develop the ability to delay gratification. But until he reaches that level of maturity, you need to understand that you are dealing with a child, for whom immediate gratification far outweighs any consequence or reward you may hold out into the future.

Many parents fail to understand this idea. They attempt to get their child's attention by adding weight to the reward or consequence. This only complicates matters. In most cases, increasing the intensity of a reward or consequence does not work. The primary factor in balancing this scale is your child's ability to cope with the anxiety or anticipation that he experiences when he is forced to delay gratification.

Adding weight to a consequence typically doesn't work. It will usually result in your feeling even more ineffective with your child and will leave your child feeling sad or angry because he has disappointed you.

Understanding that things usually get better as your child

matures can help you remain calm and become a more con-sistent parent. Furthermore, if you reflect on all three of these common parental misconceptions, your perspective will begin to shift, and you will find yourself more equipped to see what's really going on when your child tries to manipulate you to get what he wants.

The Three Innate Desires That Lead Most Parents to Inconsistency

The Tools of Power are very effective in manipulating parents because they play on the three innate desires that most parents have for their children:

1. To keep their child safe

2. To look out for their child's future interest

3. To ensure that their child is happy

As long as these three desires are satisfied, parents report that they feel quite comfortable in their role as parent. But when one of these desires is compromised, they become uncomfortable in their parenting role. Unfortunately, the mechanics of parenting often conflict with at least one of these three innate desires. Setting a limit or delivering a consequence often goes against a parent's desire to ensure his child's happiness. Obviously, your child will not be happy with a punishment or with not getting her way. And if your child is like most kids, she will do a good job of demonstrating how unhappy she is and attempt to get her way by resorting to her Tools of Power. As a result, parents feel anxiety when the Tools of Power force them to choose among their three innate desires. Out of fear of placing one of these desires in jeopardy, parents find it all the more difficult to deliver consequences and remain consistent with their child.

Your child uses her Tools of Power either to get what she wants or to avoid suffering a consequence. Her Tools of Power are intended to push your emotional buttons so that you will alter your behavior to her benefit. Although she is unconscious of your three innate desires, she has learned through trial and error that using a Tool of Power will make you uncomfortable and pressure you to give in to her wishes. She probably doesn't know *why* it works, but she knows it works.

The only solution here is for you, the parent, to learn to better cope with your own level of discomfort. Whenever you deliver a consequence or set a limit or boundary that your child contests, you will be forced to choose among your innate desires. It is impossible to be a responsible parent and always make your child happy with your decisions. For this reason, you may comfort yourself by *prioritizing* these innate desires rather than striving to satisfy all three at once.

Your top priority should always be *keeping your child safe*. If an innate desire has to be compromised, make sure that it is never this one. If she is not safe, your child may never benefit from your other two desires. For example, if you have made it a rule that your child can't ride her skateboard without wearing her helmet, no amount of resistance—"I don't like it!" "It's too hot!" "It looks funny!"—should make you bend that rule. Her safety is at stake.

The second priority should be to look out for your child's best interests for the future. This means guarding her health and welfare and making sure she is well educated—not immediate priorities to most children.

Making your child happy is, of course, important, but it is a distant third to the first two priorities. A child's emotions are fickle. Your child may yell at you and tell you that you are the worst parent in the world one moment, only to say how sorry she is and how much she loves you minutes later.

Parents are very often exploited by their child's use of the Tools of Power because they are shortsighted. They want their child to be happy, and they can't cope with her discontent. This emotional weakness on the part of the parent leads to manipulation by the child. The parent actually accedes to the child's wishes, hoping to alleviate the immediate tension in the relationship. And in the short term, it works: Any child is happy when she gets her way. But by giving in to parental anxiety and succumbing to their child's manipulation, parents may put the other two innate desires at risk. Giving in to your child when you know that you shouldn't jeopardizes your child's safety and teaches her the wrong lesson about rules and authority; this goes against her best future interests.

The following scenario is an example of innate desires giving way to a child's manipulation, and the disordering of priorities:

PARENT (emphatically): No, you can't go to Billy's house. You have to study for your test tomorrow.

CHILD (beseeching): But Billy got a new trampoline, and he said I could be the first one to try it.

PARENT (still firm, but weakening): If you study first, then you
can go.

CHILD (whining): But then it will be too dark, and I can't go.

PARENT: It'll just have to wait.

CHILD (crying): You don't want me to have fun. I could
study later.

PARENT: Don't cry; you know how that upsets me.

CHILD (more crying): But Billy is expecting me, and now you
won't let me go.

PARENT (visibly shaken by the child's tears): Okay. Okay. You
can go now, but you have to promise to study for the
test right after dinner.

This parent has given in to a primary Tool of Power:
Emotional Blackmail. Because she can't bear to see her child cry,
she has set the innate desire to see him happy above the more
important goal of protecting his best interests for the future. To
placate the child—to make him happy in the moment—she has
set him up for possible failure in school the next day. The child
has won in the short term, and the parent has lost to a Tool
of Power. What's more, the child has learned that Emotional
Blackmail works, which will lead him to use it again.

These are normal struggles that all parents go through. If you
experience these struggles with your child, it doesn't mean that you
are a terrible person, even if your child tries to make you feel as
though you are. It's simply a reflection of the fact that parenting is a
difficult task, perhaps the most difficult one you will ever face.

Read on, and you will discover ways to handle this type of situation when it comes up; and later in the book, you'll learn strategies for phasing out this type of manipulative behavior altogether.

PART TWO

YOUR CHILD'S TOOLS OF POWER

The 17 Ways Kids Manipulate to Get What They Want

In this part, I will explain the seventeen Tools of Power and give the formula for how you, the parent, can most effectively respond to your child's use of these tools. Each tool is followed by a countermeasure that I have found in my practice to be effective. When you find yourself manipulated by one of your child's Tools of Power, try the countermeasure. At first you may not recognize the tool until after the transaction has taken place. But after you sharpen your skills, you will see the tool coming, and you will be able to launch the appropriate countermeasure before it's too late. With practice, you will become more effective in setting limits and boundaries with your child and will avoid falling prey to his manipulation. It is then that you will take back the power in the relationship, guiding your child in a way that truly preserves his best interests.

3

Emotional Blackmail

Emotional Blackmail refers to your child's deliberate demonstration of a specific emotion that she knows will cause you discomfort. During this process, your child will also assert or imply that you are responsible for the way she is feeling and that the only way she will feel better is if you allow her to have her way. When your child engages in Emotion Blackmail, she relies on tapping into your emotional discomfort. Think of the expression "tugging on your heartstrings."

Emotional Blackmail can be accompanied by such outbursts as "I am so mad at you!" or "I don't care what you say!" or "You're the worst mother in the whole world!" Or your child might use such nonverbal cues as crossing her arms in protest and refusing to look at or talk to you. More often than not, Emotional Blackmail is manifest as anger, but it can also come out in subtler ways, such as in the following encounter:

CHILD (with tension in voice): But, Mom . . . I can do my homework later. I just want to see this show. It's a new episode.

MOTHER (firmly): You always say "later" and later never happens. Now turn off the television or there will be serious consequences.

CHILD (beginning to pout; on the verge of tears): You're so mean. You never let me do anything. You are ruining my life over some stupid TV show.

MOTHER (concerned): That's not true. You get to watch television all the time. Your homework only takes you a few minutes. If you start it now, you should be able to see the end of your show.

CHILD (crying): Yeah, right. You don't care about me. You just like to see me miserable.

MOTHER (attempting to comfort): Why would you say that? You know that I love you and I want you to be happy. But you have to do your homework.

CHILD (persists in crying and begins to curl up in a ball): Just leave me alone. You don't care!

MOTHER (continuing to comfort): Come on, Devin. Stop crying. It's not that bad. I'll even help you get started on your homework.

CHILD (crying intensifies): It's not bad for you, but it's horrible for me!

Clearly, Devin is playing his sad tune with the intention of putting pressure on his mother to eventually give in and allow him to watch his television program. From his mother's reaction, it is also clear why Devin relies on this Tool of Power. Her plea for him to stop crying and her offer to help him start his homework reveal her own vulnerability. Whether it is instinctual or calculated, his reaction dovetails perfectly into his mother's weakness. He effectively exacerbates the anxiety she feels in seeing him upset. He knows that if he can cause her enough discomfort, she will eventually give him what he wants in order to reduce her own anxiety.

Children tend to use Emotional Blackmail with parents who find it difficult to tolerate emotional discontent in their child. Whether it comes in the form of sadness or harsh feelings, parents who are most vulnerable to Emotional Blackmail are those who have trouble distancing themselves from their child's emotional displays. Children are very quick to pick up on this vulnerability, and they become adept at using it to their advantage when they are not getting what they want. Emotional Blackmail is a powerful tactic designed to pressure you, the parent, by ratcheting up your own discomfort.

To combat this tactic, you first need to realize that taking too much responsibility for your child's emotional outbursts weakens your position. Your own sensitivity can be used against you. Besides, children can embellish and even fake emotions. This is not to say that your child's sadness is not genuine. She may truly feel sad. But when a child is emotionally invested in getting what she wants, a parent must question the sincerity of an emotional display. More often than not, when your child is upset with a limit or boundary that you have set, her anger or sadness is on display to manipulate you rather than to secure nurturance.

You must also keep in mind that you will never be able to completely protect your child from feeling anger or sadness. It's a part of life. Your job as a responsible parent is to make decisions that keep your child safe and ensure her best interests, even if it means she is upset by your choices. In addition, setting these limits now will allow your child to strengthen her ability to cope with the strong emotions generated from not getting her way.

[COUNTERMEASURES]

The first step in neutralizing Emotional Blackmail is to avoid taking responsibility for your child's *assertions about her feelings*. This may at first seem harsh, but it is sound advice. Your child will inevitably be sad or angry at many moments throughout her life, and in the case of Emotional Blackmail, you will be unable to change your child's feelings of anger, sadness, or grief without giving in to her manipulation. But if you do give in, you are only making your job harder (and her behavior worse) in the long run because you are teaching your child that her Tool of Power really works. This will only encourage her to use it again.

In the example above, Mother might have responded by saying, "I'm sorry. I know you're upset, but you need to do your homework before you watch television." Be prepared. Children who use this Tool of Power best are fully aware on an instinctual level that any empathetic statement like this may come from the parent's desire to smooth things over. And this is precisely what the child doesn't want. Therefore, you may get a response like "You're not sorry. You don't care. If you did, you'd let me watch the show."

I don't want to devalue what you go through emotionally during such encounters. It is painful to hear your child say something like "I hate you." But bear in mind that your child is trying to manipulate you. The H word is not a true indication of her feelings about you, and in fact, your child is oblivious to how much her statement hurts you. She is using anger or sadness simply because she has learned from prior experience that it works. It is up to you to prove her wrong.

The second step in responding to Emotional Blackmail is to *stick to your guns*. Work on developing the skill of presenting yourself to your child as if you are unaffected and unmoved by his remarks. Consider the example above. Mother might respond to Devin by stating: "I understand that you think I'm ruining your life by making you do your homework, but you still need to do it before you watch television." This is the only way to curtail the hurtful outbursts. Experience shows that those parents who are able to maintain poise and composure notice a correlation between their nonresponsiveness and their child's decreased use of Emotional Blackmail as a Tool of Power. Your consistency will cause him to abandon an ineffective tool, and he will be forced to try another tactic. And since he's a clever child, he will indeed find a tactic that will work—that is, until you, the aware parent, recognize and neutralize it.

[4]

Punishment

Punishment is the name I have given to the Tool of Power in which your child deliberately attempts to provoke you into feeling emotional discomfort: anger, worry, or sadness. By using this Tool of Power, he is seeking to even the score for a perceived injustice—usually a limit or boundary you have set, or your simply not letting your child have his way.

Children's punishment styles vary. Some kids seek to make you worry. They may yell at you and say they are going to run away because "you're unfair." They pack their bags, tell you how sorry you'll be, and stomp out of the house, only to hide in the bushes down the street for as long as they can bear.

Punishment can also be used to make you feel sad, as in the case of a former client and her son. Thomas was an eleven-year-old who, for Mother's Day, had made his mother a paper heart on which he had written "I Love You." When he and his mother came to see me in my office, Thomas's mother told me that he became angry because she wouldn't drive him to see his father. (The parents had been divorced for two years.) Thomas had entered her bedroom and picked up the heart that he had given her. With the heart in his hands, he approached her and said, "Here's what I think of you!" and tore it to pieces. As his mother told the story, her eyes began to well up with tears. Days after the incident, she was still saddened. Thomas understood how to punish his mother, and he did it well.

As we talked about the reasons why he did what he did, I could see that he felt pretty bad. In our meeting, I asked Thomas for an explanation. The conversation follows:

THOMAS (obviously upset): I haven't seen my dad for two weeks, and it was the only time I could have seen him until next week.

ME (empathetically): It sounds like you really wanted to see him.

THOMAS: Yeah. But she wouldn't take me.

ME: How did you feel when she wouldn't take you?

THOMAS: Mad.

ME: Mad?

THOMAS: Yeah.

(SILENCE.)

ME: Why did you tear up the heart you gave your mother?

THOMAS: I don't know . . . Because I was mad at her.

ME: Were you trying to show her you were mad or were you trying to hurt her?

THOMAS: Hurt her.

ME: Did it work?

THOMAS (looking over at his mother, who is fighting back tears): I
    guess.

ME: How are you feeling about it now?

THOMAS (somberly): Bad.

Children can respond to their emotions impulsively and hurt-
fully. Thomas wanted to see his father. He missed him. Because
Thomas felt sad and angry that his mother would not take him
to see his father, he sought to *even the score* by inflicting the
pain he felt on her. And it worked.

Although Punishment can be used to elicit feelings of sadness
and worry, most children use Punishment to provoke their parent into feeling anger. Such is the case with Sam, a ten-year-old
who wanted his mother to buy him an M-rated video game.

Sam's mother acquiesced to buying him almost anything he
wanted. She said that she did this to prevent him from "blowing
up." She failed to understand that her overindulgence was creating a monster. Before one of our sessions, I heard Sam and his
mother arguing in my lobby. As we began the session, I asked
what the argument was about.

SAM (angry): Because she's stupid!

MOTHER (obviously frustrated): And you think that's going to
    get you the video game?

ME: What video game?

MOTHER: Sam wants this new video game, and I don't
    think it's appropriate.

SAM: You've bought me other video games that are worse
    than this one. What's the big deal?

MOTHER (becoming more frustrated): Will you let me finish?

SAM: No. You're stupid!

MOTHER (ignores Sam's comment and looks at me): I told Sam that I would get him any game that didn't have an "M" rating, but he insists that he has to have it.

SAM: I have other "M" games!

MOTHER: You do?

SAM (begins to berate): You're such an idiot.

MOTHER: Sam, don't talk that way to me.

SAM (as if tuning her out): Shut up, you're stupid.

MOTHER (looking at me): You see what I have to deal with?

SAM: Shut up, you stupid bitch! (Looks at me.) You see what I have to deal with?

MOTHER: That's it . . . I've had it. There's going to be no video games at all.

SAM (as if unaffected by her consequence): Shut up. You're so stupid!

(I should note that in normal therapy sessions, I would usually intervene before parent-child interactions became as venomous as this one. But in this case, it gave me a rare opportunity to observe how explosive things got at home for Sam and his mother. And for the purposes of this book, it serves as an example of how extreme Punishment can get.)

Sam is angry because he feels entitled to a video game. His mother typically buys him what he wants. As a result, he expects to get this game as well. For most children, expectation develops very quickly into a sense of entitlement. Sam was denied something he felt entitled to, which made him angry, which led to his use of this Tool of Power (Punishment), which would even the score with his mother by making her angry. As you may well know firsthand, Punishment can be used quite effectively.

Children typically understand very simple ways to frustrate and anger their parents. Some children become disrespectful and swear at their parents, and some become very provocative and defiant. In the most extreme cases, children may become violent and break things. Parents need to be able to differentiate between extreme forms of Punishment and all other forms of Punishment before any countermeasure is employed.

[COUNTERMEASURES]

Extreme forms of Punishment are those behaviors that are violent or physically aggressive. Breaking things or attempting to hurt someone are the most commonly observed extreme forms of Punishment. Because these behaviors are rare, let me say a few words about how to deal with them, and then we'll move on.

If your child engages in these types of behaviors, I encourage you to put this book down and seek help immediately. Your pediatrician may be the best source for a proper referral. Many psychologists and psychiatrists are trained to deal with these dangerous situations. Do not go this alone. Without the proper help and guidance from a professional, the problem is likely to get worse.

In my practice, I strongly encourage parents who see this type of behavior to visit their local police station to find out how the police would respond to a call about a child's violent behavior. As hard as it may be to think about, you may actually have to call the police to your home. Don't tell your child you are doing this. When police are actually called to the home, I have found that they are usually very good about separating the parent and child and talking to each to get a good understanding of the situation. Sometimes parents are lucky enough to arrange a visit from an officer who has a knack for working with tough kids.

But never use this type of intervention as a scare tactic. The child may see through this and realize that you fail to effectively follow through. Police are also less likely to respond to a real emergency if you have a record of calling in false alarms.

I have found that in most cases where parents have called the police once, there was never another need to do so again. In these cases, the child was awakened to the fact that the parent meant business. In most cases, the child never tests this limit again. Of course, parents need to know that they should not rely on such a tactic for every situation in which they become upset or frustrated with their child. This kind of confrontation with official authority can be particularly unnerving for a child and may produce confused feelings about the parent and the parent's feelings toward him. However, when the behavior is consistently extreme, such an extreme countermeasure usually gets results fast.

Once parents feel comfortable that no harm will come to them or their child, they find it easier to tell their child that breaking things or hurting others will not be tolerated in the home. In addition, they find it easier to let their child know that when things get out of hand in a violent manner, they *will* call the police. If traditional therapy and efforts like these fail to prove effective, children may be more amenable to more intense therapeutic programs (such as sleepaway camps or residential treatment programs).

Although you may find useful community resources, you

must remember that of the three innate parental values, maintaining safety should always be the first priority. If you feel that your child is so out of control that he may cause physical harm to himself or others, you must seek immediate professional help. Find a psychologist if you're not already seeing one.

We can now address the more common and manageable forms of Punishment.

The first step in reacting effectively to Punishment is to remain poised—that is, don't become emotionally engaged in the drama. Of course, this is easier said than done, but remember that your child will only be *rewarded* by an emotional reaction on your part. He is deliberately provoking you. He wants to see you react. Your reaction is the evidence he needs to know that he has been effective in his attempt to even the score. Stoicism rules here.

The second step in dealing with Punishment is to make clear to your child that his behavior is unacceptable. You can be kind and sensitive or you can be very firm, but you must make your expectations regarding his behavior very clear: "I understand you are upset, but you are not allowed to act this way." If your child insists on continuing to engage this Tool of Power, consider saying: "Acting this way will not get you what you want, but it will force a consequence." Hopefully, you have taken the time to set in place a consequence for this type of behavior. If you have, this would be a good time to remind your child what it is. If you have not, let your child know what the consequence will be if he continues.

Remember Step 1 and stay as poised as you can when you make statements like these. Avoid saying things like, "I really don't like it when you act this way," because these kinds of statements only tell your child that you are being affected by his actions. Such a statement validates his attempt at Punishment. Remain calm and *speak only to your child's behavior, not to your feelings*.

In some cases, children do not respond to the first two steps, and you may want to evaluate how effectively you have handled them. If you are confident with your efforts regarding these steps, you may be ready to advance to Step 3.

In the third step of dealing with Punishment, you turn the tables on your child by making his behavior work against him. You can do this through the use of a restriction. (When imposing a restriction, follow the five steps found in the appendix.)

After you have completed the steps, you are ready to use the restriction intervention. If you find that you have employed the first two steps and your child persists, make a calm, clear statement to your child that you will begin to restrict a privilege. This can be done by looking at your watch and subtracting two minutes from the privilege for every minute he continues, or you can count to three (giving ten seconds between each count) and subtract ten minutes every time you get to three.

I am quite sure that your child will find this process unpleasant. After all, you are making his behavior work against him. But keep in mind that *none of this will work if your child knows he is upsetting you*. Upsetting a parent is a very powerful and gratifying experience for a child who is trying to even the score. So stay calm and have confidence in what you are attempting to do. It is the best chance you have of curtailing this behavior.

Master this countermeasure, and you will be better equipped to face the many other challenges to come.

[5]

Shutting Down

Shutting Down is the manipulation strategy in which your child attempts to avoid dealing with an issue by simply not responding. In some cases, your child might respond to your requests or directives by simply saying "okay," but in other cases, he may not respond at all. Shutting Down is an avoidance strategy. The thought behind Shutting Down is "eventually, she'll either forget about it or stop asking." Burying their heads in the sand like ostriches often works for children.

When addressing this Tool of Power, I think of a former client, Jason, and his father. Jason loved to read. He was nine years old, and his parents had divorced a year before our office visit. The divorce is significant because Jason's father was afraid of becoming too firm with him. In previous meetings, Jason's father told me that he didn't feel that his ex-wife was supportive of his relationship with Jason—that she undermined the relationship in her talk with the boy. As a result, he was afraid that if he was too strict with the boy, he wouldn't want to see him on the court-determined weekend visits.

In this triangular relationship, the father was afraid that what the mother said about him made it easy for Jason to Punish him by canceling visiting days. This delicate dynamic played itself out on a summer morning in my waiting room.

As I opened the door to invite Jason and his father into the session, I saw Jason reading a children's magazine. He seemed to be so engrossed that he failed to acknowledge my presence. In the past, this had been a sign that the two had been fighting before the session. Here's how it went:

FATHER: Jason, Dr. Swanson's here.

(JASON continues to read and fails to acknowledge Father's remark.)

FATHER: Are you going to say hello?

(JASON continues to read. No response.)

FATHER (sits quietly for a couple of seconds while looking at Jason and then turns to me and laughs): So, how are you doing?

ME (smiling): Good. And you?

FATHER: Good. We went to see that *Star Wars* movie last night, and I think Jason might be a little tired still.

ME (smiling): Oh. Okay. Hey, Jase, what are you reading?

JASON (refusing to look at me): Nothing.

ME: I knew you would like that magazine when I ordered it. It has a lot of puzzles in it.

(JASON remains silent.)

ME: So are you ready to get started?

JASON (looks at me): Is my dad coming in?

ME: Should he?

JASON: No.

ME: Okay. Then I guess he isn't.

JASON: Okay. (Stands up and walks into my office without looking at Father.)

As Jason and I began talking, I learned that his father was upset because Jason had a tough time getting out of bed for the session. Jason believed that his father was going to want to be in on our meeting so that he could tell me about it, and he didn't want this because he hated to hear about things he did wrong. Jason reported in session: "They complain about each other so much that the last thing I need to hear is about how I screwed up. I just wish they'd be happy." So Jason's Shutting Down was an attempt to avoid having to deal with his father's complaints.

Children who use this manipulation strategy usually do so unconsciously. They simply don't want to do what they are being asked to do. As a result, they fail to respond. Shutting Down is used when a child is either asked to do something he doesn't want to do, such as picking up after himself, or asked to stop doing something he doesn't want to stop, such as turning off a video game in order to come to the dinner table.

Many of the parents I work with report that they have to ask their child countless times to pick up after himself or take the trash out. They will often ask me something like, "What is so hard about picking up his shoes and bringing them to his room?" My response is usually "Nothing." This is often followed by the question, "Then why doesn't he do it?" To which I respond, "Because he doesn't want to." In some cases, I will even challenge parents with a statement like, "Why should he pick up after himself? He doesn't need to." Frustrated by both their child's behavior and my provocative response, parents will often ask me what they should do about this problem. The solution is relatively simple.

[COUNTERMEASURES]

Parents usually have themselves to blame when their child Shuts Down. The child Shuts Down because it works—and it works because she has learned from prior experience not only that it delays her having to complete the task she is averse to but also that her parents will not deliver a consequence if she fails to respond to what is being asked of her. Simply put, the child has learned that if she doesn't want to do something, she doesn't have to.

Before we discuss the countermeasure to Shutting Down, let's discuss normal childhood development. To truly understand why children behave the way they do, one must look into the mind frame of a child. Children like to do what is fun and gratifying. "Responsibility" is a word that many children can define but with which few can identify. Chances are that you have provided certain luxuries for your child. For example, your child doesn't have to worry about putting food on the table. Your hard work and responsibility make it possible for him to operate without this responsibility. Adults don't have that luxury. In fact, we have many responsibilities, and if we don't live up to them, we and our family pay a serious consequence. Children do not look at life this way, and they probably won't do so until they become adults.

School is another venue in which we see that child's mind frame at work. Children under the age of thirteen typically don't see the significance of getting good grades in school. They simply want to impress the adults around them, and good grades are an avenue to that end. Success in school is foremost in talks I have with parents about responsibility. Granted, there are some children who innately have a passion and desire to do well in school. But if you have a child like this, keep it to yourself. It's a good way to irritate the rest of us. Most parents say that their children do their schoolwork because it is expected of them and they don't want to get into trouble when they go to class or have their parents upset with them. In some cases, children report that if they don't do their homework, they will be benched during recess and lunch at school until they make up their missing assignments. Though parents are often appalled at this naive attitude, it offers great insight into what motivates children.

Simply put, children would rather play or have fun than have to do work. And without limits and boundaries, that is exactly what they will do. This is what it means to be a child. It is the epitome of the "I Want It Now" (I-WIN) mentality. You really need to appreciate this level of development to be effective with your child. Understanding normal child development will help you avoid responding with frustration and anger. And it will help you rely on the most appropriate countermeasure—a consequence.

What is most effective, and my private practice bears this out, is to use a *contingency-based system*. Parents need to observe their children and identify what they hold as dear or sacred. Television, video games, phone time, the use of the computer, or playing outside might be some of the things your child loves most. Parents must determine the activities that most appeal to their child and schedule them in a restricted and measurable time period. Be explicit: "Video games are played in our home between five p.m. and six p.m." Once you have done this, you can begin to use the contingency system. To explain this system, let's use the example of a child who has to be asked countless times to take out the garbage.

In this case you, the parent, would tell your child that video games are played for one hour per day—no more. You would inform your child that video game time starts *only* after he has completed the necessary schoolwork. In addition, if you have to ask him more than twice to take out the garbage, he will lose ten minutes of video game time. You don't remove all of the video game time at once because that would limit any leverage you have after that. Furthermore, children are made just as uncomfortable by losing ten minutes of time as they are when they lose it all. You also inform your child that ten additional minutes will be lost for every time you have to ask him to take out the garbage again. You might prompt him with a one-sentence statement every ten minutes thereafter.

If you have done a good job of identifying the privilege that your child enjoys the most and have remained consistent with your contingency system, you will be amazed at the mastery your child gains over taking out the garbage. Shutting Down no longer works for your child. Not taking out the garbage becomes a source of anxiety. You have put the choice in terms your child cares about and can relate to—and as a result, you will see a big change in his behavior.

Though we've used the example of taking out the garbage to explain what is meant by a contingency system, you can easily draw from this example to include any form of Shutting Down you choose to target.

Of course, there are more examples, and perhaps even more challenging tricks up your child's sleeve. Read on for more manipulative strategies and how to counteract them.

[6]

Irrational Logic

Irrational Logic is a strategy by which your child attempts to soften your reaction to a particular behavior or action by introducing irrelevant information into the discussion. This tool can be employed by your child in an attempt to get what he wants, or it can be used to escape having to take responsibility for his behavior. Most parents find Irrational Logic amusing because it is fairly easy to see through, it isn't very persuasive, and it is one of the more benign of the Tools of Power.

Irrational Logic comes in two forms: self-preservation and inspiration. The self-preservation form refers to your child's attempt to reduce the seriousness of any consequence he prompts. In the inspirational form of Irrational Logic, your child attempts to persuade you to let him have his way.

A few years ago, I had a seventeen-year-old client named Kim.

She was a strong-willed and impulsive girl who was at a stage in her life where she was struggling for acceptance by her peers and would often engage in risky or inappropriate behavior in order to gain that acceptance. She would frequently violate curfew and sometimes sneak out of the house after her parents went to sleep. Kim provides an example of the self-preservative form of Irrational Logic.

I would often meet with Kim and her parents to discuss conflicts at home. She would refer to her parents as "too strict," while her parents were perpetually worried about her safety. Kim was an attractive girl, and her father feared that she could get into trouble with some of the more aggressive boys at her school. In fact, in her math folder he had found notes in which two boys propositioned her for sex.

At one of our weekly sessions, Kim's mother confronted her about the previous Saturday when she had stayed at a friend's house without calling to let her parents know about it. Here is how the conversation went:

MOTHER (obviously upset): She just didn't come home. She didn't call. She didn't tell us ahead of time. She didn't show up until Sunday. We were petrified.

KIM: God, Mom. You guys are always overreacting. I was at Tara's. It's not like I was out with a bunch of guys all night.

FATHER (upset): How are we supposed to know that? A call would have been nice!

KIM: I tried to call you guys, but I didn't get reception.

FATHER (facetiously): Tara doesn't have a phone?!

KIM (rolling her eyes): God!

FATHER (looking at me in frustration): "God." That's what I get. I should just tell her she can't go out. That way there won't be any more problems.

(MOTHER sighs. Seeing that her social life may be threatened, Kim begins to talk more but directs her words to Mother.)

KIM: Why are you guys getting so upset? It's not like I'm out doing drugs or having sex with a bunch of guys. If you don't believe me, you can test me.

MOTHER (trying to remain calm): We shouldn't have to test you, sweetheart. You should just call so we know where you are.

(ANGRY, Father responds to Mother's statement.)

FATHER: Don't you get it? She never calls. She doesn't care how you feel. She only cares about her friends. We need to stop letting her go out!

(MOTHER sighs and looks at me.)

ME: Kim, can you understand why your parents are so upset?

KIM: Yeah, but they act like I'm doing drugs or something. I don't even hang out with those kids. All we were doing is watching movies at her house.

ME: I understand that you feel that you were safe, but do you understand what it must have been like for your parents?

KIM (unyielding): They were worried because I didn't call. But we just watched movies. It's not like we were doing anything wrong.

As you can see, Kim can be quite strong-willed. The real issue was her failure to come home or to call and let her parents know

where she was. Any parent would be deeply concerned under
these circumstances. But Kim had a different thought in mind.
She was concerned about the consequence she would receive,
particularly if it involved any restrictions around her social life.
In order to diffuse her parents' legitimate concerns, Kim introduced irrelevant information. Drugs, sex, being out all night
with boys—Kim knew that these were her parents' fears, but
they weren't the topic of discussion. The only reason Kim introduced them was to avoid paying a consequence for her inappropriate behavior. This is an example of the self-preservative form
of Irrational Logic.

The inspirational form of Irrational Logic reminds me of my
marriage proposal to my wife. While I was shopping for engagement rings, a cagey jeweler showed me a 2.5-carat diamond ring,
despite my making it clear what I could afford. When I balked at
the price, he then stepped down to the 1-carat diamond—which
looked meager in comparison. Anyone who has gone through
such a process will tell you how manipulative such a tactic is,
but they can also tell you which ring my wife wears on her finger
today. Kids use this same method to get what they want, but
they reverse the jeweler's tactic.

Through Irrational Logic, a child attempts to argue that
what she wants is really not a big deal at all when compared to
the other scenario she presents (the 2.5-carat ring). An example:
the child who argues that "all of the other kids are getting com-
puters for Hanukkah. All I am asking for is a PSP." In this case,
the child is arguing for a PSP (handheld video game system).
She is using Irrational Logic to argue that the PSP really isn't
that big of a deal, especially when you consider what the other
kids are getting from their parents. Teenagers may even argue

that their curfew should be extended by conjuring up the other children in their school who don't even have to return home at night (sometimes the 2.5-carat diamond is fabricated especially for the occasion).

Whatever the form, the logic is irrational because the issue at hand is the limits and boundaries that you, the parent, have set in place for your child, and your child's willingness to adhere to them. It really doesn't matter what allowances other parents make for their children. It is irrelevant how late other children can stay out. And it doesn't matter if your child's peers are stealing, doing drugs, drinking alcohol, or ditching school. The only things that really matter are the limits and boundaries that you set in your home and your child's respect for them.

[COUNTERMEASURES]

The countermeasure for Irrational Logic is quite simple: Don't take the bait.

Many parents fall into the trap of going along with the Irrational Logic itself. Most parents can see though the faulty logic right away. But it is a safe assumption that frustration will follow any attempt at discussing the logical fallacy. This only complicates things. Your child already knows what she has done. And if she can't get away with it, she might choose to use another Tool of Power, Punishment. Dwelling on your child's faulty logic is a good way to open yourself up to being punished by her. If you insist that your child admit her mistake, she will intuitively know that a good way to punish you is to maintain her position and frustrate you by not giving you the satisfaction of validating your concerns. Don't waste your time and energy explaining the error of your child's ways. She already knows what she's doing or what she has done. If she didn't, you wouldn't be subjected to the Irrational Logic in the first place. Remember: *Don't take the bait.*

If your child points out all the ways that sneaking out of the house could have been worse, respond by saying, "We're not talking about what could be worse. We're talking about you sneaking out of the house." If she argues that she should be given a toy or privilege because her peers have been given the same, you respond by saying, "We're not talking about your friends. We're talking about what I can afford." Or, "I set the appropriate time for you to come home, and it is ____ p.m." Though your child may continue to try to make you discuss or entertain the irrelevant assertions, let her know that you will not bite.

Many parents in my practice ask me if it is ever appropriate to discuss their child's desire for more freedom or bigger toys. I respond by identifying two distinct situations: (1) when their child *is* emotionally invested in self-preservation or getting what she wants, and (2) when she *is not* emotionally invested. I then tell parents that it is okay to discuss these issues with their child when she is not emotionally invested. For example, you might discuss the issue of curfew with your teenager when she doesn't have plans for the weekend as opposed to when she is going to a party Friday night. When your child is emotionally invested, you will not have a satisfactory discussion. We will address this matter further in the next chapter, when we discuss the Tool of Power called Negotiation.

Negotiation

Negotiation is the process by which your child attempts to get his way through striking a deal with you. This manipulation strategy is usually an easy one to recognize because your child will use a statement like, "If you let me _____, I will _____." Although Negotiation can involve your child completing his end of the bargain *before* he gets his way, most often he will attempt to offer a promise or a guarantee to perform his end of the bargain after he gets what he wants. Negotiation will usually involve your child attempting to convince you, the parent, that your reluctance to give him his way is without merit. But it may also be manifest by your child attempting to offer you something that you would like from him in exchange for your giving in to his wishes.

Trevor, a ten-year-old, was brought to me by his parents, who worried over his lack of motivation. Trevor's parents were concerned that he didn't care about his performance in school. Trevor resisted doing his homework. His mother reported, "It's like pulling teeth to get Trevor to do his homework. I think he might have that ADHD thing going on." After examining her concerns in greater detail, it became quite clear that Trevor was a master Negotiator. This became very apparent during a session in which Trevor wanted to use the second half of our time together to play a game with me. (I usually divide therapy sessions in half when working with children. We spend the first half working on our goals, and if the child is productive, he can play during the second half.) I watched as Trevor persuaded his mother to give him the playtime he wanted.

TREVOR (obviously frustrated): Okay, Mom. I know. You've said it twenty times now. This is taking away from my half!

MOM: Well, obviously twenty times isn't enough or else we wouldn't still be having the problem.

TREVOR (becoming even more frustrated): Okay, Mom! God! How long do we have to talk about this?

MOM (looks at me): This is exactly what I get at home. He won't do his homework, and he gets angry at me when I ask.

TREVOR: I do my homework!

MOM: Really.

TREVOR (pouting): Yes. Can we stop talking now?

MOM: Well, I'd like to hear what Dr. Swanson thinks.

(I look at Trevor, and the room falls silent.)

TREVOR (breaks the silence after about ten seconds): Okay, look. You want me to do my homework when I get home

before I watch TV. If you just stop talking about it, I'll
do it. Okay?

MOM: What does that mean?

TREVOR: It means I'll do my frickin' homework. Okay?

MOM: So what you're saying is that as soon as you get
home, you will sit down and complete your homework without me having to ask you over and over and
over again?

TREVOR: Yes!

MOM (obviously feeling as if she is getting somewhere with him):
For how long?

TREVOR (getting more frustrated again): I don't know! A week,
okay?

(MOM looks at him expressionless.)

TREVOR (still frustrated): So can I have my half now?

MOM: Is this a deal?

TREVOR: YES!

MOM: Okay.

(MOM gets up to leave the room and gives him the time he wanted.)

Wow! He was good. And she fell for it. Trevor had man-
aged to get his second half despite having failed to complete
his homework as his mother had asked him. Trevor wanted to
play a video game in the second half of our session and he knew
his mother was frustrated. He also knew that she desperately
wanted him to complete his homework without a fuss. So he
used Negotiation to get his playtime. He offered his mother
a promise that he would change his behavior in exchange for
twenty minutes of playtime.

So the question that begs to be asked is: Did he live up to

his promise? No. Trevor's mother returned frustrated to the next session, complaining that Trevor had kept his promise for two days after the last appointment, but after the weekend, "He was back to his old self again."

[COUNTERMEASURES]

The trick to responding to Negotiation is to remember that talk is cheap.

The first step in counteracting Negotiation is to make sure that you get your end of the bargain *before* your child receives his. Your child may be very genuine in his intention to fulfill his part of the bargain when he makes the deal, but getting him to follow through may prove to be quite difficult. Without the incentive to perform the behavior he has promised, your child will most likely become more resistant to completing the task when he is asked to do so in the future. When this occurs, it only leaves you frustrated and feeling as if your child has lied to you. In the case of Trevor and his playtime, Trevor's mom could have intervened more effectively if she had responded to him by saying something like, "I know you want to have some time to play, but you haven't earned it yet. Maybe this week you'll do your homework and you will be able to play the next time you see Dr. Swanson." By saying this, she would have made sure that she received her side of the bargain *first*, and the Negotiation would not have been doomed to failure.

The second step in responding to Negotiation is to remember the three innate desires you possess as a parent and make the commitment to yourself that you will not place your child's situational happiness before ensuring her future interests. Many parents allow for Negotiation, mistakenly believing that it will satisfy both parties. But the fact is that Negotiation will often simply delay the feelings of frustration and disappointment experienced by both parent and child.

Parents often feel a more intense pressure to give in to their child's wishes when Negotiation is employed. When your child uses Punishment, it can be fairly easy to say no to your child because she is treating you badly. But when your child uses Negotiation, she appears not only to be making a responsible effort to satisfy your concerns, but to be engaging in a healthy social skill: the art of compromise. Remember, however, that no matter how wonderful Negotiation may seem, your child's best future interests should take precedence over her happiness in the moment. Chances are that your efforts to make your child happy through Negotiating will lead to ill feelings later on if you fail to get your end of the bargain first.

Simply put, Negotiation is a good idea only when your child satisfies her end of the deal before she gets her way.

[8]

Confrontation and Protest

Confrontation and Protest is the process by which your child will confront you by raising the stakes emotionally and behaviorally in order to get what she wants (you might refer to this as a tantrum). This process usually begins when a child is told no. The child becomes frustrated and her emotions escalate. The escalation may begin with whining but quickly rises to shouting. In the severest cases, children will throw or break things and attack others in addition to screaming and yelling. It's no wonder that many parents feel that the only way to calm their child down when she uses this Tool of Power is to give in to her demands. Usually these children settle down when rewarded with the object of their desire.

Alex was a seventh grader who was seeing me for behavioral problems at home and school. He had a habit of getting upset and blowing things out of proportion. By the time Alex was finally brought to me, he was on probation at school for throwing a wet piece of paper at another kid in his English class. He wasn't subtle. His friends were planning a trip to Magic Mountain amusement park in celebration of one of their birthdays, and Alex really wanted to go. Alex's mother attempted to use the Magic Mountain trip to motivate him to do well in school. She told him that he would be able to go if he stayed out of trouble at school for the two weeks prior to the trip. As could have been predicted, he blew his chances. Four days into the first week, Alex decided that it would be funny to pull another child's pants down during his PE class. But he didn't think it was very funny when, as a result of the prank, he was suspended for two days.

It should be noted that Alex's mother and father were divorced. Alex lived primarily with his mother and saw his father only infrequently. His mother was a very successful businesswoman who endured great internal conflict. She appreciated her career because it afforded Alex the opportunity to live in a nice area, attend a prestigious private school, and wear the name-brand clothes he so coveted. But she also felt guilty because her career pulled her away from her son. Alex would often use that against her by saying things like, "You're never here."

When Alex and his mother entered our session together, he was pretty upset. He often played the victim, and in this session he resisted accepting responsibility for his suspension. His focus was on how unfair his mother was for taking away his trip to Magic Mountain.

ME (beginning of session): How are you guys doing?
ALEX (pouting): Bad.

ME (concerned): Why?

ALEX: My mom won't let me go to Magic Mountain.

MOTHER (arms crossed): And tell him why.

ALEX (angry): You tell him.

MOTHER: Alex got suspended from school. (Looks at Alex.) You want to tell him why?

ALEX (angry): I'm sure you will.

MOTHER (looking at me): Alex got suspended because he pulled a boy's pants down at school.

ALEX (begins to yell): We were just playing around. He did it to me first, and I was just getting him back.

(ARMS still crossed and staring at me, Mother remains quiet.)

ALEX (looks at me): Now she won't let me go to Magic Mountain for my friend's birthday.

ME: Do you remember the deal that you and your mom made last week?

ALEX (appealing): Yeah, but that's different. We were just playing around.

MOTHER: But what was the deal?

ALEX (shouting): What do you mean, "What was the deal?" We were just playing around.

MOTHER: You got suspended.

ALEX (really beginning to raise the stakes emotionally): So what? Mr. McClanahan's a jerk. He's always looking to get me in trouble. And you believe him.

MOTHER: You didn't pull a boy's pants down?

ALEX: You're being an idiot! It was Eric, Mom, and we were just playing around!

(MOTHER is quiet.)

ME: Why are you calling your mom an idiot?

ALEX: Because she's taking away Magic Mountain for playing around.

ME: She's following through on a deal you made last week.

ALEX (appealing): But it's not like I was doing something bad. We were just playing around, and they are taking it too seriously.

MOTHER (becoming frustrated): I'm becoming too serious?

ALEX: You all are!

MOTHER (even more frustrated): Okay, fine, Alex. Go ahead and go to Magic Mountain, and I'll just stop caring! And if you flunk out of this school, then you can just go to public school and we'll see how happy you are there!

It was at that point that Alex succeeded . . . temporarily. He was able to work over his mother to the point that she simply gave up the fight. However, it didn't end up that way. Later in the session I intervened by strongly suggesting that the mother follow through with the deal. As much as Alex did not like my suggestion, I explained to him that I thought it would be in his best interest because it is situations that cost us a lot that end up allowing us to grow and to think before acting.

This problem will not go away by giving in to your child's wishes. Giving in only encourages your child to use this Tool of Power again in the future. Remember: *Kids do what they do because it works.*

I must also point out that the children who use Confrontation and Protest as their primary Tool of Power often have one or both of the following issues in common. Some seem to be born with a difficult temperament, and parents will even report that their child "has been this way since the day he was born." Research has demonstrated that genes do have a lot to do with our behavior and emotions, and some temperaments indeed seem to be consistent from infancy. In these cases, parents need to understand that this is part of the child's makeup. Though interventions can improve the situation at home, parents of these children must accept that they are raising a challenging child. Parents raising a challenging child may feel a sense of disappointment and failure if they do not come to terms with these assertions. Please understand that the prognosis is not doom and gloom; it's just not smooth sailing.

The second characteristic shared by some of the children who use Confrontation and Protest is that they are often paired with parents who are emotionally distant. Such emotional distance can derive from many sources, such as parental depression, a distant relationship that the parent had with his own parents, working too much, or even marital discord. But whatever the cause for the emotional distance, children may seize upon it and exploit it. Children who tend to rely on Confrontation and Protest may not understand why it works, but they have learned what their parents cannot tolerate and know that their parents will usually give in when they raise the stakes emotionally or behaviorally.

Sadly, it is the children in the second circumstance who tend to pick up on the emotional distance of their parents and find a redeeming pleasure in getting what they want. The object of their desire almost becomes a pseudo-replacement for the love they are missing from the parent. Often, the distant parent of such a child is unable to cope with the child's emotional and behavioral outbursts and, disregarding long-term consequences, gives in to the child's demands in order to feel closer, to feel like a good parent, or to avoid further Confrontation and Protest. The impact of a parent giving in or backing down to the child's Confrontation and Protest can be devastating for the child because he is led to assume that limits and boundaries in the world are pliable. In addition, the child will most likely experience a sense of guilt and a blow to his self-esteem for pushing his parent into a corner. Even though the child gets what he wants in the short run, he is well aware that his means for getting it were inappropriate and most likely hurt others he cares about.

[COUNTERMEASURES]

The countermeasures to Confrontation and Protest vary. That is to say, they differ depending on the intensity of the Confrontation and Protest that your child exhibits. To make it easier, let's divide the levels of intensity into three types: (1) whining and moaning, (2) screaming and yelling, and (3) physical aggression against objects and people. After discussing the basic countermeasure for this Tool of Power, I will make additional suggestions for parents whose child falls within the latter two categories.

If the most your child does is whine and moan, breathe a sigh of relief. This is normal behavior and indicates that you may have the opportunity to become even closer to her. For example, your child is swimming in the pool, and you want her to get out, dry off, and get ready for dinner. When you tell her this, your child responds with, "No, Mom, I don't want to get out. Just give me five more minutes." Your response should be something like, "I know you're having a lot of fun and I wish you could stay in the pool, but you need to get out now." If your child continues to whine and refuses to exit the pool, you should stay calm and express one clear point about the consequences of not following your directive, such as, "I've asked you to get out of the pool, and if you're not out by the time I count to three, you will go to bed a half hour earlier tonight." After making this statement to your child, count to three over a period of forty seconds. You do this by waiting ten seconds after you give your directive and say, "One." If your child doesn't respond over the next ten seconds, say, "Two," and so on. If you reach three and your child has failed to respond, deliver the consequence. You can also chip away at the things your child loves to have access to (pool, computer, video games, and so on). Most preadolescent children respond well to this method. For teenagers, you may have to use money or the phone as a motivator. Regardless, you chip away at the privilege. (See the appendix.) Never take it all away at once because you'll be left with nothing more to take, and your child may become so frustrated that she won't care what you do. In these cases, she will just want to get back at you and may purposely not respond as a means to this end, resulting in another Tool of Power: Punishment.

Whether or not your child responds by the count of three, always praise her for following directions. Even if your child complies after you reach three or, after not complying, serves the punishment you set, you can make statements like "thank you for listening to me" or "good job." These statements are well received by children.

If your child resorts to screaming and yelling, you know all too well how difficult this can be to tolerate. But nonetheless, you should attempt to follow the guidelines I have laid out above. Though the child's behavior is more intense, she may just need to be reeled in a little.

Of course, your child may be exhibiting these behaviors as a result of your failure to remain consistent in the past. If this is the case, counting and chipping away at the things she loves will be upsetting to her because she's not used to it. However, you might want to take a closer look at your child. Her screaming and yelling may indicate that something more serious is going on than the simple frustration of not getting her way. If the triggering situation does not warrant the response you've received from your child, it may mean many things. For one thing, a child who suffers from feelings of sadness or anxiety has low tolerance for things not going her way, and not getting what she wants may trigger an eruption of emotions.

A child who screams and yells at you may be saying something to you about the quality of your relationship with her. Perhaps she is reacting to a feeling that you are never around, and the least you should do is offer her something to feel good about when you are not there. Of course, most children are not aware of the compounding factors behind such complex dynamics, so they wouldn't come out and say this to you. The only thing your child might tell you is that you're not giving her what she wants or that your consequence is unfair.

An intense response could indicate a lower tolerance because of life circumstances, such as divorce, the death of a loved one, being left out by friends, or even an act of terrorism. Nevertheless, I would strongly encourage you to discuss your child's use of this Tool of Power with her when she is not emotionally invested in getting her way. If you find that your child is guarded around these issues, I would encourage you to seek help from a pediatric psychologist. Doing nothing about it can lead to things getting worse for you and your child.

Finally, if your child resorts to aggression (for example, hitting and throwing or breaking things), seek help immediately. My goal here is not to put the fear of God into you, but you need to know that this type of behavior is not normal. The reasons for this behavior can be as simple as immaturity or an inability to verbally articulate frustration adequately. The behavior could have to do with family dynamics, or could even occur as a result of an actual impairment. When I say "impairment," I am referring to everything from a learning disorder to a mood disorder or attention deficit disorder. Because you, as a parent, are a part of the system, you will not be able to figure out all the dynamics that go into this explosive form of behavior. It will take a very skilled professional to understand all the intricacies that contribute to explosive behavior in your home.

Forgoing this advice and using the methods I have indicated for the first two forms of Confrontation and Protest may make things worse for families with children who exhibit this most intense form of behavior. And things can get much worse in these situations.

It is my belief that whenever there is conflict between a parent and a child, it can go one of two ways: It is either resolved or unresolved. A marital therapist once told me that he always encouraged the couples he worked with never to go to bed angry. He felt that this was very damaging to a relationship. I support this belief in parent-child relations. When a conflict arises, and they do occur in every family, it needs to be resolved. It doesn't matter if it's at the end of a confrontation or later that night. When a conflict is unresolved, your child will personalize it. This is because your child does not have the ego strength to parent himself and say, "Look, I know Mom and I got into it, but I know she loves me and she knows I love her, too." Now I am not saying that your child doesn't know that you still love him. But what I am saying is that the process of going to bed sad or guilty as a result of a conflict takes a big toll on your child.

Leaving these issues unresolved will have a negative impact on your child's self-esteem as well as on his future behavior. Kids who don't feel good about themselves will take it out on those around them—specifically the ones who love them. Resolve all conflicts through communication and an expression of your love for your child.

Under the most extreme conditions—including when your child refuses to respond or talk to you—at the end of the day, you must always reassure him that you love him.

9

Steamrolling

When your child incessantly badgers you to get what she wants, she is using the tactic of Steamrolling. And when she doesn't succeed with endless variations on the theme—"Come on, Mom. Please. I really want to go"—this tactic can turn into an attack or criticism: "You're so unfair. Just let me go."

Steamrolling is perhaps the most common of all the Tools of Power. Every parent can recall the multitude of times his child has said, "Just let me have it. Come on! Just this one time. Why won't you let me have it? You never let me have it. Come on. Just let me have it." The pleading persists, and it seems that your child doesn't hear or understand the word "no." But the reality is that she not only understands the word "no" but knows how to turn it into "yes."

Such was the case with thirteen-year-old Blake, whose parents brought him to see me over this very issue. A young master of Steamrolling, Blake had a prolific repertoire he would bring to the table. On one occasion, Blake wanted to go with friends to ride motorcycles in the desert. He didn't own a motorcycle and had never even ridden one, but he said that one of his friends had an extra one he could use. Understandably worried for his safety, Blake's mother adamantly opposed the trip.

Before this particular session, Blake's parents said he had gotten better at accepting no for an answer. But this session provided what psychologists call "a response burst" (the return of an undesired behavior). Notice how this progresses:

ME: So what are you guys planning for your spring break?

BLAKE: I don't know. I want to go to the desert and ride dirt bikes, but my mom won't let me.

MOTHER: Yep. I'm the bad guy. I told him I'd think about it, but I just don't think it's safe.

BLAKE: But it is safe, Mom. What's not safe about it?

MOTHER: Blake, you have never even ridden on a motorcycle. You're thirteen. You don't even have your driver's license yet.

BLAKE: It's not illegal. Kids can ride motorcycles there.

MOTHER: It's not about that.

BLAKE: Well, what's it about?

MOTHER: Blake, we've already discussed this, and I'm not going to change my mind.

BLAKE: We haven't discussed this. You just told me no.

MOTHER: Okay, so you have your answer.

BLAKE: But that's not fair. Dad thinks I should be able to go. You're the only one who doesn't want me to go.

MOTHER (looks at me): Oh well . . . Here we go again. (Laughs.) And we were doing so well.

BLAKE: I have been doing well. That's why you should let me go.

(LEANING back in her seat and looking toward the ceiling, Mother remains silent.)

BLAKE: Mom, that's not right. I've been working really hard. Even Dr. Swanson said I've been doing a great job. It's not fair that I can't go. All my friends are going, and I'm the only one who can't. You just worry too much. Why should I work so hard if you're not gonna let me do the things that I want to do?

(NO response from Mother.)

BLAKE (looks at me): Is it fair that my dad doesn't care and my mom says I can't go?

ME: I understand your point. But it kind of sounds like you're Steamrolling again. I don't think this is going to get you what you want.

BLAKE (frustrated): Nothing will work with her.

(MOTHER smiles.)

ME (noticing that we have reached the end of the session): We have to wrap up.

On the way out, I winked at Blake's mother for her steadfastness. Although he attempted to Steamroll here, Blake had actually become far less dependent on this tool thanks to his mother's resolve. She had said that in the past such interaction would go on for hours. Blake fought tenaciously to get what he wanted. But as evidenced in our session, his mother had become increasingly adept at identifying the tool and remaining calm and resolute. To her credit, as soon as she saw the Steamroller coming her way, she simply stopped talking about the subject. Blake would try other tactics, such as Tactical Engagement and Character Comparison (we will discuss these Tools of Power in later chapters), but she stuck to her guns and remained consistent. Blake's progress was proof of that.

Unfortunately, many parents do give in to Steamrolling. If a parent is exhausted from a long day at work, not feeling well, or simply tired of the fight, giving in becomes the easiest alternative. But giving in exacts a price: more manipulation in the future. As with any of the Tools of Power, giving in only proves to the child that the tool works.

[COUNTERMEASURES]

The two countermeasures to Steamrolling are quite simple: (1) do not give in, and (2) find a way to make your child's Steamrolling work against him. That's not to say it will be easy. There is no magic formula for remaining calm and firm, and that is going to be your greatest challenge when responding to this Tool of Power.

"Kids do what they do because it works" is a dictum that might well be turned into a refrigerator magnet, and it clearly applies to Steamrolling. It is up to the parent to make sure the tool doesn't work. The fact is that if you don't give in to your child, he will eventually abandon the tool because it doesn't work.

Giving in to your child when it is against your or his best interest is counterproductive to ensuring his best interests in the future. Every child needs to learn that no means no and not "no, unless you keep badgering me." Your child needs to be able to adapt to and recover from disappointment. If he doesn't learn this skill early on at home, he will be destined for failure later in life. Life is full of disappointments. Children who do not learn to adapt are at a higher risk for anxiety and depression. No matter how worn down you may feel, it is imperative that you focus on the child's long-term benefit and not give in.

With this tool, one sometimes has to carry the response a step further. Without something to lose, some children will Steamroll for hours.

The second step in responding to Steamrolling is to use what I call the Two Minutes for One Minute Rule. With this method, you take away two minutes of something your child enjoys doing for every minute she continues an inappropriate behavior, thereby making her own behavior work against her.

To use the Two Minutes for One Minute Rule, consider the things that your child craves or desires. Once you have your list, regulate the things. You do this by placing a time frame around the access your child has to each of these things. For example, if your child loves video games, determine a block of time when video games may be played. You might tell her, "Video games are played between five p.m. and seven p.m. on weeknights. Not before and not after." Outside those times, unplug the game controllers and put them away. Once you have set rules controlling the activities your child enjoys, you can begin to use those rules to your advantage. Let's discuss how.

Sit with your child and explain that when she Steamrolls, you will ask her to stop. If she continues, check your watch, signaling to her that you will be initiating the Two Minutes for One Minute Rule. From that point, she will lose two minutes of her video game time for every minute she continues to Steamroll. Some children prefer to have you give a verbal prompt in addition to looking at your watch. I see nothing wrong with that. Just make sure that your prompt is simple and clear and without room for negotiation.

Two cautions: First, set these regulatory periods (such as video game playing) at the end of the day so that you have something up your sleeve throughout the day, and second, if you find that your child fails to respond to the steps for longer than six weeks, either revert to ignoring the Steamrolling or find another activity to regulate.

It is particularly important to meet with your child at the outset of this scenario. Answer any questions she may have and make clear your expectations and the consequences of her behavior. This meeting will reduce confusion and frustration. Mystery is not part of the disciplinary technique. You have nothing to hide here.

Throughout this process, it is important that you resist getting caught up in an emotionally charged power struggle. This is particularly challenging when the child is Steamrolling. There are three things you can do to avoid a damaging power struggle with your child.

First, you must become adept at identifying when your child is using her Tools of Power. You should be able to name the Tool of Power when she uses it. Assigning a label increases your power and puts you in control. If you can name it, you can counteract it. In this case, you should be able to say to yourself, "My child is trying to Steamroll me."

Second, remind yourself that no matter how heated the interaction, you will be far more effective if you remain calm. If you are not in control of yourself, then you will not be in control of the situation. In addition, if you allow your emotions to take over, you will become vulnerable to another Tool of Power, such as Punishment. You will also send a signal to your child that things are going her way. Conversely, if you remain calm, your child will sense that you are in control. You are the gatekeeper. Don't leave the gate wide open by succumbing to your emotions.

Third, trust in the power of consistency. Don't escalate consequences when your emotions are aroused. Consequences must be logical and predictable. If they are fueled by your emotions, they will only seem arbitrary and unfair. Trust in the Two Minutes for One Minute Rule and stick to it.

Don't drop your guard. Some trickier ploys are just around the corner.

10

Covert Operations

Covert Operations include lying, stealing, deception, and with-holding information. There are two forms of this tool. The first form is any secretive attempt by your child to get what he wants from you. The second form is his attempt to avoid a consequence through lying, deception, or withholding information.

Parents find Covert Operations to be one of the most deceit-ful of all the Tools of Power. But if your child employs these strategies, it does not mean that he operates from a moral void. Although Covert Operations may seem underhanded, sneaky, and corrupt, children who use this Tool of Power do so impul-sively or because, in the moment, it seems like the best way to get their needs met. Most of the children who use this strategy do not think of the long-term consequences, nor do they con-sider the feelings of others. For younger children, any Covert

Operation is a primitive strategy that is relied on for the same purpose as the rest of the Tools of Power: manipulation.

Chris was a fifteen-year-old whose parents brought him to me because of his disrespectful behavior. He was particularly disrespectful toward teachers and others in positions of authority, but the parents were personally bothered by the way he treated them.

An added feature of this case is that Chris's parents were very critical of him. Other professionals working with this family were puzzled by the intensity of criticism in the home because outwardly, the parents were the models of social grace.

But this is not to excuse Chris's inability to recognize social limits and boundaries. He was masterful at using words to escape accountability for his actions. Chris was very good at Covert Operations.

During one of our sessions, we invited Chris's father in to join us because Chris had often referred to him in my office. The session went fairly well. The two connected on a number of critical issues in which they had clashed in the past. However, the issue of honesty, which Chris's father took very seriously, came into question that night.

In an ongoing attempt to make Chris accept responsibility for his actions, his father tried to curb his son's spending habits. Chris's father had asked him to document the purchases he made in a journal, and in a dialogue that started with schoolwork, he asked him about his journal.

FATHER: I think it's very important that you follow through with your responsibilities. There is no reason that you should be getting a C in English. The only reason you're getting a C is because you're not doing what you're supposed to.

CHRIS: That's not true, Dad. I just have to turn in my project and that's worth forty percent of my grade. Once I get that in, I'll have at least a B.

FATHER (looks at me): I mean this is the thing. Chris always gets himself into a position where he's playing catch-up.

CHRIS: That's not true. I'm getting A's or B's in every other class.

FATHER: History?

CHRIS: Yeah.

FATHER: I thought you were missing work there, too.

CHRIS: I turned it in Tuesday.

FATHER: But it was still late.

CHRIS: Yeah, but it's not a big deal. I still got full credit for it.

FATHER (looking at me): Well, I just don't understand it. Why is it so hard for Chris to just turn in his work and do the things he's supposed to?

ME: Have you seen any improvement?

CHRIS: Yes!

FATHER: Can I talk? (Pauses.) He asked me. (Pauses and looks at Chris silently for a few more seconds. Then he looks at me.) Chris has gotten a lot better at doing his work, and we've told him many times that we're proud of him. I just don't want to always have to be on him. I mean, at what point will he just get it done himself?

CHRIS: I am getting it done.

ME (looking at Father): So you're really worried about him. You want to make sure that he learns the things he'll need to know to be successful in life.

FATHER: Well, yes. And I hope Chris knows that. (Looks at Chris.)

(CHRIS remains silent.)

FATHER: One of the things we started doing is to have Chris write down what he spends his money on. (Looks at Chris.) Have you been doing that?

CHRIS: Well, not every day.

FATHER (suspiciously): What do you mean "not every day"?

CHRIS (frustrated): I mean I haven't done it every day.

FATHER: Well, how many days have you done it?

CHRIS: I don't know.

FATHER: What do you mean, you don't know? We just started this a week ago.

CHRIS: I haven't thought about it.

FATHER (tension rising): Well, have you done it at all?

CHRIS: I mean, I got my journal.

FATHER: Have you written in it?

CHRIS: No.

FATHER (frustrated, he sighs and looks at me): This is what I'm talking about. Chris likes to play games with his words so you never know what he's up to. (Looks at Chris.) Why is it so hard to just be honest and say, "I didn't do it"?

Chris was very good at deceiving others through playing with his words. It just so happened that his father was better at picking up on it when it happened. Chris used Covert Operations with his parents because, as he said, "I'm tired of hearing their complaints." Instead of taking care of his responsibilities or taking the time to sit down with them and talk it out, he relied on this primitive strategy.

Although in this case, Chris developed this strategy as a method of dealing with a critical family dynamic, I have found that several factors are associated with children who tend to rely on Covert Operations as a favored Tool of Power. In particular, Impulsive Children tend to use this Tool of Power more often than children who do not demonstrate this trait. This is because the Impulsive Child is more likely to act before thinking (see Chapter 23). In addition, Impulsive Children tend to get themselves into trouble more often and are aware of the reputation they have earned. In these cases, lying may not be used so much to avoid a consequence as to avoid having to be confronted by the disappointment of their parents.

In my practice, there is a clear correlation between Covert Operations and family situations in which parents do not spend much time supervising and attending to their children. I believe a big reason children resort to Covert Operations is that they are used to the freedom that comes from their parents spending little time with them. They are not used to being questioned as often as children who spend more time with their parents, and they may impulsively attempt to deceive their parents in order to protect their level of freedom and escape consequences.

Finally, teenagers often use Covert Operations in an attempt to gain more control over their lives and live up to the expectations of their peers. In order to find their own identity, they must rebel against the messages or preferences of their parents. Adolescents often tell parents either covertly or overtly, "Let me do it my way." Because teenagers are more likely to engage in risky behavior, parents are not so quick to accede to that freedom. But many teenagers quickly learn that they can get away with "doing it their way" and may have a reasonable chance of avoiding a consequence if they simply deceive their parents.

No matter what the reason for Covert Operations, you will find the countermeasures that follow to be helpful.

[COUNTERMEASURES]

There are two steps in responding to Covert Operations. The first is to remain calm and think rationally; the second is to deliver a consequence that is fitting and effective.

Normally, parents have strong emotional reactions when confronted with Covert Operations. When they learn that their child has intentionally deceived them, they feel angry and frustrated. Curb your emotions. If you become emotionally involved, you will only risk becoming the victim of another Tool of Power. Remember, *the Tools of Power are designed to push your emotional buttons*, and often your reaction is precisely the gratification your child is seeking.

It is far better to stay calm and exact a consequence, keeping the focus on your child's inappropriate behavior rather than on your emotional reaction. Remember that he is employing a tool to get what he wants. Covert Operations are rarely used as a personal attack on a parent. Chris serves us as a perfect example. He didn't want to have to document all of his purchases; he saw no reason for it, and in a previous session he complained to me about how much work it would be. But he also didn't want to get in trouble with his father. Although Chris's father was frustrated with the word games he played, he would be wrong to assume that Chris purposefully betrayed his trust. He just didn't want to do what he was asked to do.

The second step is to deliver a fair and logical consequence. Keep in mind that when you deliver a consequence for Covert Operations, it should be distinct from and in addition to any consequence you give for the original inappropriate behavior. In Chris's case, he would suffer a consequence for failing to complete the journal (the original inappropriate behavior) and an additional and separate consequence for his attempt at deception (Covert Operations). As it turned out, Chris's father did just that. After our meeting, Chris lost his allowance for the following week—a consequence for not journaling—and in addition, he had to write a letter to his father apologizing and explaining how lying can damage relationships—a consequence for the deception. (I had previously suggested to Chris's parents that his lying was likely prompted by the intensity of criticism within the home.)

When thinking of an appropriate consequence for Covert Operations, I often encourage my clients to use the Principle of Restoration, which means having your child do something to compensate for the damage he has done. It's not unlike a husband bringing his wife flowers after speaking harshly to her earlier in the day. When using this intervention, I instruct the parent to explain to the child that lying is very damaging to a relationship because it hurts others and distances you from the person you lie to. The child should be told that a restorative action would show the person he lied to that he does value the relationship.

The father's creative use of restoration was to make Chris

write him a letter of apology. You can choose any restorative tasks you wish. But keep in mind that they should be predictable, delivered in a calm fashion, and discussed with the child prior to any attempt at Covert Operations.

The reason I like this approach is that it lets your child know that no matter how badly he may have behaved, he can work to repair it. It also suggests that no matter what happens, you will still love him. I also like it because children genuinely do feel guilty when they know they have upset you, and giving them a task to make it up to you empowers them to feel better about themselves.

Finally, I should point out that every child lies. You must understand that it isn't an indication of your child's lack of moral character. It's a desperate tool of the immature. Don't be too critical of the child or of yourself. Stay calm and help him restore the relationship. That, after all, is what you both want.

As you read ahead, remember that the goal is always for better parenting and a happier family life.

[11]

Divide and Conquer

Divide and Conquer is the very familiar strategy with which your child attempts to get what he wants by exploiting weaknesses in your relationship with your spouse. Divide and Conquer comes in two forms. In the first form, your child takes advantage of poor communication between you and your spouse. In the second form, your child attempts to use a difference of opinion between you and your spouse to his advantage.

A child's attempt to exploit the lack of communication between you and your spouse is the most common form of Divide and Conquer. Your child understands which parent is most likely to give him what he wants, and when communication between parents is strained, the child uses that to his advantage. Jared is a sixteen-year-old I have worked with who is the personification of Divide and Conquer.

Jared came to see me because of what his parents called "an

anger issue." Jared was prone to angry outbursts in which he swore at his parents, and he never did what they asked. In my office I had the opportunity to see Jared in action. It was early on in treatment, and his parents had come in to discuss their frustration. This is how the scene unfolded:

JARED (to me): I don't see why they have to come in with me. This is supposed to be my therapy.

FATHER: You know why we're here.

ME: Why are you here?

FATHER: Well, Jared went out with his friends Friday to a concert that I specifically told him I wasn't sure about.

JARED: But you weren't home.

FATHER: Jared . . . That doesn't matter. You knew I was going to look into it.

JARED: Yeah, but you weren't home, so I asked Mom.

FATHER: Jared, that's bullshit. The only reason you asked your mom was because you knew we hadn't discussed it.

MOTHER: Larry, there's no need to swear.

FATHER: No need to swear? There's no need to undermine me when I told him I'd look into it.

MOTHER: And I'm supposed to know that the two of you had this talk? Nobody told me.

FATHER: You could have called and asked.

MOTHER: But how was I supposed to know that you wanted me to call you?

FATHER: He knew!

ME (looking at Dad): So you told Jared you would give him an answer later, and (looking at Mom) you had no idea that they had talked about the concert.

MOTHER: No.

ME: Jared, why didn't you call your dad if you knew he was going to give you an answer?

JARED: He was at work.

ME: Okay, but why didn't you just call him?

JARED: Because my friends were over and they wanted to go.

ME: So you asked your mom instead of your dad?

JARED: Yeah.

ME: What do you think your dad would have said if you called him?

JARED: I don't know. He was at work.

ME: Your mom?

JARED: She doesn't care. She just wants to know where I'm going.

FATHER (looks at me): Exactly . . . Did you hear that? He knows she doesn't care. That's why he asked her.

Jared's father finally understood. And after further discussion, so did everyone else. Jared didn't want to admit it, but he knew we were on to his game.

Jared knew which parent would give him the answer he wanted. And he also knew that his mother would not think to call his father. This was a constant in their relationship. But it was soon after this meeting that both Jared's mother and father made it a point to work on improving their communication.

In the second form of Divide and Conquer, when your child exploits a difference of opinion between you and your spouse, he will take the side of the parent who is most likely to give him want he wants. In the example above, Jared reported that his mother was more amenable to letting him go places with his friends. If he were to have employed this second form of Divide and Conquer, he might have stroked his mother with a statement like, "Thank you for understanding, Mom. Dad's too strict." Jared was sensitive enough to avoid using this tactic in our session. His father's reaction would have likely been explosive. But this tactic can be very effective.

Families who don't communicate are often victims of this tactic, and divorced parents are particularly susceptible to it because of the physical separation. Children are very quick to pick up on breaks in the family dynamics that they can use to their advantage. It is an opportunity that is too convenient for some children to resist.

[COUNTERMEASURES]

The countermeasure to Divide and Conquer requires two steps. They are, first, nurturing a clear and consistent communication with your spouse and, second, dealing out consequences. There is a third suggestion I will also offer.

Divide and Conquer is only effective when there is a breakdown in communication. To avoid being manipulated by this tool, you must work on that communication. Parents often point out that it is impossible to discuss every little thing that comes up. And I agree. Luckily there is a way around this dilemma.

I tell parents in my practice that they should do two things to avoid becoming Divided and Conquered. They must first sit down and discuss the types of decisions they want to share. Jared's father wanted to be involved in the decision about where his son could go on weekends. It would be a good idea to make lists of the types of decisions that you want to share. Besides where the child gets to go, you might want to have a say in how much money you spend on purchases for him or whether or not he can have a sleepover—all potentially contentious issues.

After reviewing both of your lists, you may choose to modify them. When you feel comfortable that both lists are complete, combine them into one list. After composing your list, make a pact that you will always consult each other before deciding on the issues on the list.

Second, don't be afraid to tell your child, "Let me think about it." What seems urgent to your child need not be urgent for you. If your child pleads that time is of the essence, then she simply hasn't planned effectively. She hasn't given you ample time to make a decision. But remember, it is still the parents who make the decisions. Tell her you have to think about it, then honor the pact and check with your spouse.

Delivering consequences is also important. Although Divide and Conquer is quite different from Covert Operations, the two share a common feature: They both are damaging to mutual trust. Jared circumvented his father and went straight to his mother because he knew she would give him the answer he wanted. As a result, the father felt both undermined and betrayed.

Because of the damage that Divide and Conquer inflicts on relationships, I suggest that any consequence be restorative in nature. As we discussed in the last chapter, restoration is the process by which your child performs a behavior that is designed to restore the damage done by his attempts at manipulation. Keep in mind that any restorative consequence is given in addition to a consequence for the original inappropriate behavior. In the case of Jared, his parents should provide a consequence for his going to the concert without his father's permission (the original inappropriate behavior) and an additional consequence for his decision to use Divide and Conquer.

Providing a predictable consequence for his manipulation makes the child aware of the risk at hand should he choose to employ Divide and Conquer. In Jared's case, he now has to have permission from both parents before he acts. This is the consequence of his playing one parent against the other.

In conclusion, consider the fact that your child is manipulating by exploiting a weakness in your relationship with your partner. Parents often feel that they are to blame for these types of problems because they have failed to communicate effectively. In addition, the parent who told the child she could have what she wanted is likely to feel uneasy about imposing consequences. These are understandable reactions, but they do not excuse your child from behaving inappropriately. She knows what she is doing. And when she chooses to use this Tool of Power, she places a higher priority on getting what she wants than she does on honoring the relationship that you share with your spouse or co-parent. Keep that in mind. Just because you failed to communicate with your spouse or told your child she could have what she wanted doesn't mean your child is innocent. Understand this and follow through with the two steps I have laid out above.

Parenting is a team responsibility.

[12]

Tactical Engagement

In Tactical Engagement, your child plays emotional games to lure you back into an argument that you had hoped was settled. It is a Tool of Power she engages after you have made a decision and are walking away. It is timing that separates this from Steamrolling. While Steamrolling happens *during* the child's plea, Tactical Engagement occurs *after* you have given your "final" answer.

Every child understands that the only way to get what she wants is for you to consider her argument. And she is understandably frustrated when you tell her no. The cleverest of children know how to rekindle the discussion.

A few years back, I had the opportunity to work with a grand master of Tactical Engagement. Usually parents initiate visits to my office, but Kevin, seventeen, brought the family to me. In our first session, he said that the reason he made the appointment was that his parents were habitually anxious and fearful for his welfare. He also said that they always sought his opinion about things that he didn't want to have to think about. At one point, when his grades and social life were precarious, his parents had asked him if he would like to move to a neighboring city so that he could change high schools. This rightfully perplexed Kevin. The parents were abdicating adult decisions to a teenager.

Our first few sessions were filled with stories of parental anxiety. I decided to set up a meeting with the parents alone, and it turned out that they had a moving tale to tell. Before Kevin was born, they had had two other children. The first child, a girl, drowned in their swimming pool at only six months of age. A few years later, they decided to have another child, but this one, a boy, was stillborn. Kevin's life was preceded by tragedies that left a pall over the family.

Kevin was unplanned. He was conceived a year after the death of the second child. His birth was haunted by the specter of death. In my office, Kevin's mother said, "Every morning I breathe a sigh of relief when I see him awake and alive." Their anxiety was compounded by their feelings of guilt over the death of their first child. Both had arrived at pool's edge shortly after the infant had fallen in, and they did everything they could to rescue her. But both had also perpetually blamed themselves for not doing enough. Though the parents are educated and rational in most matters, they thought of the death of the second baby as punishment for their carelessness.

When I heard this family history, the Kevin puzzle came together. How could they not help feeling anxious and insecure as parents?

After that meeting, I scheduled a session with the whole family. I thought that it was important for Kevin to get an accurate perspective on why his parents behaved the way they did. But the session took an unexpected turn as I saw Kevin use his parents' guilt and anxiety to his advantage. He did this through Tactical Engagement.

ME: Hi, guys. Thanks for coming in. (Looking at Kevin.) I know I didn't talk to you about this earlier, but after meeting with your parents, I thought it would be good for all of us to get together so that we could come to a better understanding of why we do what we do.

KEVIN: That's cool.

ME: Great. (Looking at parents.) I'm really happy that we had the chance to meet because it helps me understand a lot of the things Kevin has talked about.

(BOTH parents smile.)

ME (looking at Kevin): Do you mind if I tell your parents some of the things that we've talked about?

KEVIN: Go for it.

ME (looking at parents): You know, I think one of the things that is hard for Kevin to understand is why you decide to include him in many of the decisions you make that have to do with him.

KEVIN: And other stuff.

(PARENTS nod.)

ME: Kevin often talks about how he wishes you guys would make decisions without his approval.

MOTHER (looking at Kevin): Is that true?

KEVIN: Yeah.

MOTHER: But you often don't like the decisions we make.

KEVIN: Like what?

MOTHER: What did you bring up on the way in here?

(DAD smiles.)

KEVIN: What are you talking about?

DAD: The iPod . . .

KEVIN: Oh . . .

MOTHER: Kevin has a habit of not letting things go. And on our way up here, he brought up this iPod issue again.

KEVIN: No.

FATHER: Yes.

ME: What's going on with the iPod?

MOTHER: Kevin's birthday is next month, and he wants an iPod. We said we would consider getting him one, but he has to have the top of the line.

KEVIN: That's not true.

MOTHER: No? Why don't you tell Dr. Swanson what you told us in the elevator.

(KEVIN shakes his head and rolls his eyes.)

MOTHER: Last week we told Kevin we would get him the iPod we could afford. Tonight, Kevin brought it up again. On the way in here he said that he might as well be adopted because we only get him second-rate stuff. (Looks at Kevin.)

KEVIN: I didn't say that. I said you never get me what I want.

FATHER (looking at Mother): Well, yesterday he told me that we'd be better off never having kids because then we wouldn't have to spend our money.

KEVIN: Whatever.

ME: Kevin . . . you're a smart guy. Why did you choose to use those exact words with your parents?

KEVIN: I don't know. I just want the sixty-gig and they only want to get me the thirty.

ME: No. I understand that you want the bigger iPod, but you could have simply said that. Why did you say what you did?

KEVIN: 'Cause I knew it would bother them.

ME: How?

KEVIN: I don't know . . . because they are always worried that I'm not happy.

ME: Do you know why?

KEVIN: Because they're anxious?

ME (looking at parents): Does he know what you told me on Tuesday?

FATHER: Well, he knows about Kaela [the daughter who drowned], but I don't think we told him about the still-born.

MOTHER: We told him.

ME: Does he know how it's affected you?

FATHER: I don't know. (Looking at Kevin.) Do you?

I decided to intervene at this point in the session. It was obvious that I needed to spend more time with Mom and Dad in order to help them work through their grief and to help them understand how it was affecting their parenting. However, I didn't think it was appropriate for Kevin to be a part of this. I wanted to keep this session focused on his behavior.

ME: Kevin, I think what we're figuring out is that you are very perceptive. And your parents want you to be happy. But while you say you don't want to be involved

with making big decisions, you do take advantage of
their anxiety.

KEVIN: How?

ME: Well, whether you think about it or not, when you
want something, you say things to make them feel bad
because that makes it more likely that you'll get what
you want.

KEVIN: Yeah . . .

ME: That's pretty smart of you to figure that out, but
(looking at parents) I think your parents are learning
something also. And that is that maybe you aren't
as unhappy as you pretend to be. Could that be the
case?

MOTHER (tears welling up in her eyes): I know he doesn't really
mean it, but it's so hard. (Dad puts his arm around her.) We
just feel so lucky to have him, and we want him to be
happy.

ME: I know. But he doesn't know what you've been
through. And he doesn't need to know. He just needs
to know that no means no.

MOTHER: You're right. (Mom leans into Dad, breaks down, and
cries.)

Kevin resented the fact that his parents burdened him with
their anxieties. But when he wanted something and his parents
had opposed it, he had no problem using that anxiety to draw
them back into a discussion in the hope of changing their minds.
Sadly, this only intensified their parental insecurity and led to
more of the anxiety that Kevin despised.

There are many forms of Tactical Engagement. The manner

in which it is engaged depends on the vulnerabilities of the parents. Children are aware of the hot buttons and know how to push them. If a parent is insecure, a child may say, "If you weren't such a jerk, you'd let me have my way." In such situations, the insecure parent might respond, "Don't call me a jerk. I let you do a lot of things." A child with an oversensitive parent may say something like, "I am so depressed because I can't have what I want." And the sensitive parent may respond, "You have plenty of other things to make you happy. Why do you need that?" In both of these cases, the child has figured out how to push her parent's emotional buttons to get him back into a discussion after the "final" decision has been made.

What makes Tactical Engagement challenging is that it forces parents to be aware of their feelings and to avoid allowing them to control their behavior and decision making.

[COUNTERMEASURES]

There are two steps in the countermeasure to Tactical Engagement. The first is to refuse to discuss your decision with your child once you have made it. If your child refuses to accept your decision and begins to use this Tool of Power, proceed to the second step. Point out what she is doing and deliver a consequence that is commensurate to the length of time that she continues.

First, you must make a decision, and after you have done so, tell your child what it is and make it clear that it is final. From this point on, refrain from discussing the matter further. Doing so will only encourage more Tactical Engagement in the future.

Refraining from discussing your decision may be easier said than done. After all, when your child engages in this Tool of

Power, she specifically targets the issues that she knows you will find difficult to resist. You might feel compelled to respond if you are emotionally charged. But if you respond, you are doing just what she wants.

Remain cool and calm. But if staying calm is difficult for you, you must begin to work on this shortcoming. You shouldn't need your child's validation to feel calm and in control. Resign yourself to the fact that *children will always question limits that we set.* Sometimes they do so because they don't understand why the limits are set, while at other times they really don't care about the why—they simply want their way. In either case, we need to be patient and realize that as long as the child is emotionally invested in getting her needs met, there is no—and I do mean no—opportunity to enlighten her with your wisdom. Forget about discussing the matter further or trying to explain. Such moments of clarity can be attained only when your child is not emotionally invested in getting what she wants.

At the point where you think your child's use of Tactical Engagement has gone on for too long, go to this next step: Present him with a consequence. In order to do this, you must first point out your child's behavior. Then you need to inform him that if he chooses to continue, he will receive a consequence. In Kevin's case, his parents could have responded to his comment before the session by saying, "I know you're unhappy with our choice, but we are not going to discuss it further. If you wish to continue badgering us about it, you will have a price to pay." That price is the consequence.

For younger children, the Two Minutes for One Minute Rule is a fitting consequence for Tactical Engagement—that is, take two minutes away from a desirable activity for every minute he persists. Let him know that you are looking at your watch, and make sure your prompt is simple and clear, without room for negotiation. For teens, you can use the same countermeasure, but the target may need to shift. Instead of chipping away at a desired activity, you may need to chip away at something more fitting (curfew, money, and so on).

It is particularly important to remain calm and refrain from further discussion of any decision you have made. If your child refuses to take no for an answer, a consequence may be necessary.

If Tactical Engagement sounds warlike, it is because you are in a war—a war waged between youthful desires and good parenting.

13

Creating Leverage

Creating Leverage is the process by which your child attempts to get what he wants through building up "good deed" points. His method for building up these points may vary. The two most common ways of Creating Leverage are either to remind you of all the positive things he has done or to perform a series of behaviors he knows you will appreciate before asking for what he wants. Either way, your child hopes to use his good deeds to create enough leverage so that you feel pressured to give him what he wants.

If you were to watch this Tool of Power play out in your home, you might see the following type of interaction taking place.

CHILD: Mom, I want to go over to Justin's.
MOTHER: Well, wait a minute. We're just about to sit down
    to eat.

CHILD: I'll eat at Justin's.

MOTHER: I don't know. It's getting kind of late.

CHILD: Come on. All I've been doing is working around here. I took out the trash, I mowed the lawn. And I even helped Dad fix the shelves in the garage.

MOTHER (feeling pressured): I know. You've been very helpful.

CHILD: Then you'll let me go?

MOTHER: But it's a school night, and you've got to get up early tomorrow.

CHILD: I know, Mom, but that's not fair. I would have gone earlier, but I was stuck here helping you guys.

MOTHER: Okay. What time will you be home?

In this example, the child is asking to visit a friend late in the evening on a school night. His mother knows that it goes against his best interests because he needs his sleep to perform well at school the next day. But he did help out around the house after all, and she is inclined to compensate him and give in to his wishes. In the end, the mother caves in to her child's use of Creating Leverage and places a higher priority on making him happy than on ensuring his best interests in the future. This violates the priorities of a responsible parent. Looking out for a child's best interests is more important than ensuring his situational happiness.

In summary, Creating Leverage is your child's scheme to pressure you into giving him his way by building up leverage points. Although there are many forms of this Tool of Power, the strategy of them all is to compel you to compensate your child for his efforts, often at the sacrifice of long-term goals.

[COUNTERMEASURES]

There are two important things to keep in mind when your child begins Creating Leverage: (1) the priority of keeping your child happy should never take precedence over his best future interests, and (2) *you* are the one to decide how and when to reward your child for his good deeds.

In the case above, Mother has a difficult time setting the limit for her child. It is clear that she is aware of her child's need to be well rested for school the next day. But it is also clear that she feels bad that he missed an opportunity to visit a friend because he was helping out around the house. In this case, like many others, she begins to feel guilty. Her guilt causes her to allow her child to do something she knows is not in his best interest.

A more appropriate response to this situation follows.

MOTHER: You really did help out a lot. And I am very thankful.

CHILD: Then you'll let me go?

MOTHER: I would love to let you go, but I won't let it come at the expense of your schoolwork.

CHILD: But it won't!

MOTHER: I am sorry, but the answer is no, and that's final.

Had this mother responded to her child in such a manner, it is safe to assume that he would have been upset, momentarily. But he would get over it and would eventually find another strategy for pleading his case. In the original scenario, the mother would later regret letting both herself and her son down because she didn't act in his best long-term interests. This would be harder to get over than the transitory disappointment he expressed for not getting his way.

When responding to Creating Leverage, remember that there is *no relationship between the positive things your child has done and his immediate desires*. A deal was never made—no quid pro quo. In the case above, this mother never said, "If you take out the trash, I'll let you go to Justin's house." The son was proffering a one-sided deal. And for that reason, you owe your child nothing.

It is you who decides how to compensate your child for his performance—not him. Often, saying "thank you" is compensation enough. Creating Leverage is a very clever Tool of Power because it is designed to make you feel obligated where no obligation applies.

Imagine if life were to operate this way. A car salesman might say, "Look, I took you on a test drive and spent time with you. It's only fair that you buy the car from me." This is precisely why contracts need to be made and executed *before* any action is required. One is not indebted by an assumption made by another. Without a contract, we owe the other person nothing but goodwill. And much of parenting is goodwill combined with action.

To avoid being victimized by Creating Leverage, you need to let your child know in advance that he doesn't get to choose the rewards for his good behavior. And make it clear that hidden motives are not acceptable.

When your child begins Creating Leverage, ask yourself, "Did I make a deal with my child?" If not, your child is making an attempt to use leverage to get what he wants.

Bargaining is a power play, and the power is in your hands.

14

Playing the Victim

When your child tries to get what she wants by making you feel sorry for her, she is Playing the Victim. Children can achieve this goal by simply acting unhappy. Or they can resort to asserting that you have cheated them or let them down in some way.

Regardless of the method, your child may present herself as feeling sad, frustrated, or angry in an attempt to persuade you to give her what she wants. In addition, she will do the best she can to make you believe that the only way she will feel better is if you allow her to have her way.

Lauren was a twelve-year-old girl in my practice who was a master at making her mother, Anne, feel sorry for her. Lauren's parents had been divorced for a year, and her mother was very sensitive to her daughter's anxiety over the breakup of the family. Anne was particularly affected by the fact that her own parents had divorced when she was about Lauren's age. Even though her divorce from Lauren's father was amicable, Anne often wondered if Lauren felt the same deep pain that she had felt when her mother divorced her abusive alcoholic father.

Here is a scene that unfolded between the mother and the daughter.

LAUREN: I want a new bedroom set.

ANNE (looking at me): She's been talking about this all week long. Her friend Zoe just got a new queen-size bed, and now all Lauren can think of is getting a bigger bed.

LAUREN: I haven't been talking about it all week.

ANNE: Really?

LAUREN: Well, that's just because I'm still sleeping in the same bed I got when we moved into the house.

ANNE: And what's wrong with that?

LAUREN: You mean besides the fact that I can barely fit into it anymore?

ANNE: Lauren, the bed fits you fine. You just want a new bed.

LAUREN: Dad picked that bed out, Mom. I never wanted it. And now every time I have to sleep in it, I have to think of him.

(BOTH Anne and Lauren are silent.)

ME: What do you think about when you think of your dad?

LAUREN: That he's not there anymore.

ANNE: Sweetie, he still loves you.

LAUREN: I know, Mom, but can I just have a new bed?

It was obvious that Lauren was exploiting Anne's concern for her feelings in order to get a new bed. The truth is that she really did miss her father, but her attempted manipulation of her mother made it difficult for the mother to trust the genuineness of her sadness. I coached Lauren's mother to trust her daughter's emotion when she was not emotionally invested in getting her way. That seemed to help.

Playing the Victim can be demonstrated through the fabrication of emotion (your child faking sadness or anger), or it can revolve around real-life events. But it is invariably designed to lure you into the child's emotional state so that you will give the child her way.

[COUNTERMEASURES]

The countermeasure to Playing the Victim is easier said than done. The rule to follow here is to separate the emotional content from whatever short-term goal the child is trying to obtain. Provide empathy, understanding, and nurturance, but withhold the desired reward. Every parent feels empathy for her child. Seeing your child in pain may be one of the most difficult things you will face. Nevertheless, it is imperative that you, the parent, muster the strength to refrain from giving in to your child when you know it is not the right thing to do, no matter how bad you feel for her.

Empathy is the best thing you can offer your child—better than a new bed, a video game, or a sleepover.

It is hard to remain focused on your goal when your child begins Playing the Victim—hard emotional work. But remember that your vulnerability is one of the key reasons that your child Plays the Victim. Your child knows how much you love her and that you cannot bear to see her in pain. Lauren clearly understood this.

If Lauren's mother were to have followed my advice, she would have responded as follows.

ANNE: Does it really upset you that Dad's not around?

LAUREN: Yes . . . That's why I want a new bed.

ANNE: Well, wait a minute . . . We can discuss the bed in a minute. Let's talk about your feelings first.

LAUREN: No, Mom. I don't want to talk about my feelings. I just want a new bed.

ANNE: But a new bed is not going to solve the problem. If you are upset about your father, I want you to be able to talk about it.

By responding in this manner, Lauren's mother would have been able to separate Lauren's feelings over her father from her desire to have a new bed. She would have then been able to address the feelings and provide empathy for Lauren if she were truly feeling sad. Unfortunately, because Lauren was likely using these feelings to get a bed by Playing the Victim, she would have become frustrated and continued to pressure her mother for the bed. Lauren's mother could have responded by saying, "We are not going to get a new bed right now. But if you wish to discuss your feelings, I am here for you."

In summary, when your child is emotionally invested in getting her way, you should use caution before blindly accepting assertions or actions regarding the way she feels. Express empathy but help your child separate her feelings from her goal. The new bed and the loss of the father are distinct issues that have been conflated in Lauren's mind.

You are the adult. You are in charge of separating out emotions and practical action.

[15]

Forging the Friendship

Forging the Friendship is the strategy with which your child attempts to blur the boundary between parent and child. The goal of this Tool of Power is to turn your parent-child relationship into a friendship, thereby breaking down the power structure that should exist. When you revert from parent to friend, the power dynamic shifts. A friend is less able to say no. After all, friends are always "cool" with each other.

Children who employ this Tool of Power are understandably unaware of the dysfunction between themselves and their parents. They may fall into this role because they take emotional care of a parent or because the parent shares inappropriate information with them, such as details of a dispute with a spouse or financial worries. In my practice, divorced parents are most often at risk of blurring the healthy boundary that should exist between themselves and their child.

Divorce may naturally leave a parent feeling lonely and devalued, and he may also fear losing a child's love or respect. Divorce leads some parents to feel that they must defend themselves so that their children won't think of them as the bad parent in the breakup. And loneliness caused by a separation may lead many parents to share their bed with their child or to plan more "friend-like" outings together. The parent may take the child to R-rated movies or watch inappropriate TV shows with him. She may engage in inappropriate chats with the child. She begins to treat the child like a peer. The child may seem like a good listener, and he is put in the burdensome position of taking care of the parent's emotional needs. Although this can be an uncomfortable experience for a child, many children enjoy the feeling of power that comes along with being their parent's "new best friend." Regardless, this friendship comes at a cost. Using the power the parent has given him, the child feels entitled to make decisions affecting his own life. And parents who have allowed themselves to fall into this dynamic with their child often give in for fear of losing the child's affection.

Taylor, fifteen, was what psychologists call a "parentified child," a child forced to take on the responsibilities of her parent or caregiver because the parent or caregiver is unable to provide for her emotional needs. In Taylor's case, after her father took off with her mother's best friend, Taylor was often left to care for the emotional needs of her mother as well as her own. Unfortunately, Taylor had all the information about the tangled relationship and even gave her mother advice on how to move on.

The first session we had together went like this:

TAYLOR (as if unaffected by the parents' breakup and the father's betrayal): Yeah, my dad left my mom because he was having an affair with Cheryl. She was my mom's best friend. They even went to high school together.

ME (concerned): Wow! How are you doing with all of this?

TAYLOR (nonchalantly): I'm fine . . . It's my mom that's all sad.

ME: How so?

TAYLOR: She can't even get out of bed in the morning. I have to wake her up and make her breakfast every morning. It's ridiculous.

ME: Have you had contact with your dad?

TAYLOR: No. I don't want to. He's an asshole. Look at what he did to her.

ME: Look at what he did to you.

TAYLOR (shrugs): I'm fine. I don't care.

ME: You don't care?

TAYLOR: Not really. I mean, since he left, I get to do things he would never let me do.

ME: Like what?

TAYLOR: Well, my mom let me drive here today.

ME: Do you have a permit?

TAYLOR: Not yet. My mom just had a headache and told me to drive.

The longer the session went on, the more troubling the information became. With about fifteen minutes left, I asked Taylor to wait in the lobby while I talked with her mother. The description she gave me of her mother led me to believe that she was suffering from a deep depression. I wanted to have a chance to check in with her before they left.

In my discussion with Taylor's mother, Sharon, she said she was indeed feeling depressed. And when I asked about her thoughts on Taylor's caretaking role, she reported that she was well aware of how her depression was affecting Taylor and that she had already begun her own treatment with a psychiatrist.

She then went on to describe her frustration with Taylor. Taylor had a difficult time accepting no for an answer. When I asked her to give me an example, she brought up Taylor's insistence on driving to my office for this first session. When I asked her why she let her fifteen-year-old drive, she said, "We've been through so much together. I just wanted to give the kid a break." This was a definite warning sign that the parent-child boundary, if there had ever been one, had been seriously breached. I guessed, and my hunch was later confirmed, that Sharon used Taylor as a friend to satisfy her own emotional needs. And as a result, the boundary that existed between them was erased. Taylor was her buddy, and Sharon didn't have the heart to say no to her.

When I see a child in my practice who either is too chummy with a parent or acts more entitled than he should be, I question the emotional stability of the parent. Parents who meet their emotional and intimacy needs through interactions with other adults don't need their children to fulfill these needs. Such parents are more capable of setting limits with children without fear of emotional isolation.

Because parents who fall prey to this Tool of Power are often at the disadvantage of feeling emotionally empty, it is very important to recognize the signs that can lead to a child's rely-ing on this Tool of Power.

SIGNS OF FORGING THE FRIENDSHIP

1. Parent and child sleeping in the same bed.

2. A child actively defying his parent or using such inappropri-ate language as, "Oh please, you're only saying that because he's here. You know when we get home you're not going to follow through."

3. A child referring to his parent as "cool."

4. A child who behaves as though he is much more adult-like than his age warrants, or uses language such as "those kids" when referring to peers.

5. Children saying their parents "let me get away with what-ever I want."

6. Children reporting that their parents are easy to manipulate.

7. Parents reporting that they often need permission from their child.

8. Parents setting few or no limits or boundaries.

9. Parents wanting to have fun with their child but never impos-ing consequences for inappropriate behavior because they don't want to "ruin the time they spend together" (I call this the Disneyland Parent).

10. Parents seeking advice and guidance from their child in such a way that places the child in the caretaker role.

[COUNTERMEASURES]

The countermeasure to Forging the Friendship has every-thing to do with the parent. It is very common for a child to badger a parent for more information than is appropriate. Your child may ask about why you were arguing with your spouse, what led to your divorce, how much money you make. She may even ask questions about your finances or, God forbid, your sex life. These questions arise from normal curiosity. It is this same curiosity that prompts her to ask you what you bought her for her birthday. It's normal.

But a parent is under no obligation to answer every question. Sometimes we simply need to tell our children that it isn't appro-priate for us to discuss our finances with them. Or in the case of divorce, a healthy boundary may be to say "sometimes people just grow apart" rather than telling her that her father had an affair.

Most parents can make sense of this. They have an instinc-tual awareness about what is appropriate to discuss with their child. But it's not a failure of logic that leads a parent to reveal too much. It is their coping skills that get these parents into trouble. Some parents are so emotionally needy that they rely on the support they feel they receive from their child. Some feel the need to defend themselves when a spouse or an ex-spouse has allegedly made a negative comment about them. Regardless of the cause, the countermeasure to Forging the Friendship hinges on the integrity of the parent.

As a parent, you need to do the best you can to take care of yourself and seek support from those you trust. If you suf-fer from depression, get treatment. If you feel lonely, consider age-appropriate companionship. And if you are divorced, understand that giving out too much information in self-defense can ultimately damage your child. Some parents cannot contain their anxiety. These parents feel that they have to give their child information even when they know it's inappropriate. If you fall into this category, let me suggest that you talk with your friends. If you don't think you have any friends to talk to, tell a spouse, a parent, a relative, or even a pet. But refrain from telling your child. Don't use your child as a release valve.

If you have already committed these errors and now have a child who is taking advantage of you, just be honest. Let her know that you have made some errors in judgment. Explain to your child that your inappropriate sharing of information has led to the breakdown of the healthy boundary that is supposed to exist between you. Tell her that you will work on correcting that by setting appropriate limits and boundaries in the future. If she complains that "you used to be cool and now you're being mean," you can empathize and let her know that this change may be confusing. Don't expect your child to understand why you are choosing to change your behavior. Some will honestly not understand, and others will refuse to understand in an attempt to use another Tool of Power, such as Confrontation and Protest, Playing the Victim, or Emotional Blackmail. But stick to your guns and practice integrity.

Counseling is a good resource for parents who fall prey to this Tool of Power. If you are one of these parents, it is likely that you have emotional needs that are not being met, and that is nothing to be ashamed of. Many people have emotional needs that go unmet. It's how we handle that challenge that makes all the difference.

Don't run away from depression, anxiety, or problems with intimacy. To do so will only damage your relationship with your child.

16

Character Comparison

Character Comparison is another strategy that your child may employ to get what he wants. When he doesn't get his way and he compares you unfavorably to another parent or authority figure, he is using Character Comparison. This Tool of Power is used to pressure you into giving him what he wants. The strategy is to compare you to another adult in order to point out how wrong or deficient you are.

Will was a seven-year-old client of mine who was full of anger and frustration. One of Will's biggest frustrations derived from the restrictions his parents placed on the types of video games he could play. The video game industry had begun to rate their games, with "M" standing for "mature content." Will argued incessantly with his parents over a particular M-rated game. This game engaged the player in acts of murder, carjacking, and even sex with a prostitute. Needless to say, his parents weren't buying it.

One evening, Will employed this tactic with his mother, Ruth. (His father was unable to attend the session.)

WILL (whining): I want Grand Theft Auto.

RUTH (frustrated): Oh, come on, Will. How many times are you gonna bring this up?

WILL: Until you get it for me.

RUTH: Well, the answer hasn't changed.

ME: How many times have you asked them, Will?

WILL (again whining): I don't know . . .

RUTH: I'd say over a hundred . . .

WILL: No!

ME: Have they changed their minds?

WILL: No . . . because they're idiots!

RUTH: This is what we get if he doesn't get his way.

WILL: Well, it's because you guys aren't fair.

RUTH (frustrated): Will, I told you I am not going to buy you an M-rated game. So you can either accept that or call us unfair . . . I don't care.

ME: Will, is this working for you?

WILL (whining): But it's not fair. Blake and Sean both have the game and I don't. Their mom doesn't care. (Looks at Mother.) Why do you? (Cuts off Mother's attempt to respond, and faces me.) You don't understand. They have cool moms and I don't!

RUTH (beginning to waiver a little): Oh, so because I won't get you the game, I'm not a cool parent.

WILL (defiantly): No.

RUTH (looks at me): "Well, look, I don't know what to do. If the other boys have the game . . ."

ME: All right. Ruth, what do you think is going on here?

I had to interject at this point because Will's tactic was quite clear, and his mother was going for the bait. Soon after, both Ruth and Will laughed as he identified the process. Mom eventually turned to Will and said, "You are pretty good at doing that, but I'm still not getting you the game."

In many such cases, I've listened as parents argue with their child over whether or not a friend really does have such a game. They'll sometimes say something like, "I'll look into it." In all these cases, the parent has taken the bait and fallen into the trap—the trap of buying into the child's irrelevant logic. This is precisely the child's goal when employing the tool of Character Comparison.

Many parents fall prey to Character Comparison by erroneously thinking that their child is simply mistaken or lying. Others take the bait out of a need to be liked. Regardless of the reason why, entertaining this Tool of Power is a mistake because the behavior of other parents is irrelevant to the decisions you make for your child. Will's friends may actually have this inappropriate video game, and their parents may have even purchased it for them. But that doesn't make it right for your child to have it. You make the rules in your household.

[COUNTERMEASURES]

There are two steps to the countermeasure for Character Comparison. The first is to stay focused on what is relevant—

that is, what your child is after and whether or not you will let him have it. The second step is to ensure that your own insecurities do not prevent you from setting appropriate limits for your child.

The countermeasure to Character Comparison requires you to stay focused on the real issue. In the case of Will, the real issue is whether or not his parents want him to have a particular video game. Will uses Character Comparison to move the focus from what Mom and Dad want to what other parents may do. Rather than taking the bait as Will's mother did in the session described above, the correct way of responding to Character Comparison would be to make a statement like, "I understand that your friends may have the game you want, but we are not talking about them. We're talking about what your father and I think is appropriate."

If Will were to persist with a comment like, "Well, you guys are so uncool. I wish you could be more like my friends' parents," an appropriate response would be, "You are entitled to your opinion, but it will not change our minds about the video game, and that's final."

The second step in this countermeasure is to make sure that you are secure enough in yourself that you can resist taking the bait. All parents want to be seen in a positive light by their child. Loving your child in a responsible way requires that you do not place his happiness, or at times yours, before his best interests for the future (a mantra that you should adapt as your own). Your child will continue to love you even if you say no—even if he's angry enough to say he doesn't. If you set limits and stick to them, your child will not only love you but *respect* you.

If you find that the statements your child makes hurt you too much, speak to your spouse about it. If that doesn't seem to help, seek out support from friends, and if you need to, get help from a psychologist. In order to reliably use the countermeasure to Character Comparison, you will need to be strong enough emotionally to assure yourself that your child's assertions are just an attempt to manipulate you into giving him what he wants.

There will always be times when your child says that some other parent is cooler than you. But it is better to be a good parent than a cool one.

17

Casting Doubt

By Casting Doubt, your child attempts to make you give in to her wishes out of fear that something bad may happen to her if you don't. Some children are very good at picking up on their parents' anxieties, and they almost instinctively use those anxieties to their advantage. When your child employs the strategy of Casting Doubt, she tries to make you anxious about not giving her what she wants. She will do this either by insinuating or directly telling you that there will be a horrible consequence for not going along with her plan.

Although this Tool of Power may be used to obtain a desired object or to go somewhere, Casting Doubt is most often used when your child wants to get out of doing something. The strategy behind this Tool of Power is simple: "If I can make my parents worry about the consequences of setting a limit for me, they are much more likely to allow me to do what I want."

Perhaps one of the most acute displays of Casting Doubt that I have seen involved a client I will call Tracy. Tracy's case also demonstrates how difficult it can be for a parent to be confronted by this Tool of Power.

Tracy was a seventeen-year-old girl whom I had been treating for depression. She was once hospitalized for threatening to take her own life. In our sessions, she had often reported that she never felt she could meet her parents' expectations for her schoolwork. As she started her final year of high school, she also entered into her first long-term relationship with a boyfriend. She had dated Robert for four months when the incident in my office occurred.

There was a direct correlation between time she spent with Robert and her falling grades, as documented by progress reports the school sent home. Her parents were understandably unhappy with this and attempted to limit the time she could see her boyfriend during the week. At first, Tracy seemed to respond positively to the boundaries set by her parents, and she and her parents agreed in my office that if she complied and improved her grades, she would be allowed to spend more time with Robert.

After a few weeks had passed, Tracy came to her weekly session with her father. This was a departure, because I normally saw Tracy alone. But this time, he wanted to join us. As the session began, Tracy's father reported that he had found Robert in her bedroom at two in the morning, and he was very upset.

Here is how it was recalled:

FATHER: I heard a noise coming from her room, so I went to see what was going on. When I walked in, I found him there.

(Tracy sits quietly, picking at her eye.)

FATHER: I mean, I don't know what to do. I feel like I can't even go to bed without feeling like she's going to do something like this. (He pauses, then continues.) I wanted to wait until we came here to talk about this. But last week I found a bong [a pipe for smoking marijuana] in the microwave in the guesthouse.

(Tracy is still sitting silently.)

FATHER (looks at Tracy and continues): I don't know if it's hers or Robert's, but I assume it's Robert's. I don't think Tracy uses drugs.

TRACY (softly): It's mine.

FATHER: What?

TRACY (louder): It's mine . . . Robert doesn't smoke pot.

(At this point, the room becomes silent.)

In the course of the hour, Tracy's father learns that his daughter smokes pot and that she has regularly been having sex with her boyfriend. Tracy also tells her father that her mother knows about everything. Tracy's father remains stoic, and for some time he sits silently. Then he goes on:

FATHER (looking at me): Well, I don't know what to do. I don't see anything good coming from this relationship.

TRACY (frantic): You can't make me stop seeing him.

(Father remains silent.)

TRACY (bursts into tears): You guys don't understand. All you ever do is complain about my grades and rag on my friends. I am so depressed! I feel so worthless! (Starts to sob.) I hate my life! I hate everything! Robert's the

only thing I live for. If I can't see him, I might as well
kill myself!

(There is a silent pause, then Father continues.)

FATHER: Well, I don't know what to do. (Looks at me.) I mean,
do you really think she's going to hurt herself?

ME: I never play around with something like this. If Tracy
says she's going to hurt herself, I have to believe she
means it.

TRACY (looking at me): So what, I have to go to the hospital
now?

(I am silent.)

TRACY: I'm not going to fuckin' kill myself. I just don't
know what their fuckin' problem is. (Looks at Dad.) He's
my boyfriend. You guys are gonna have to accept that
sooner or later.

Although most cases of Casting Doubt do not involve threats
of suicide, Tracy's case demonstrates how this strategy can be
effective in provoking a parent's feelings of anxiety. In severe
cases, such as in threats of suicide or physical harm, parents
should seek immediate help from a psychologist or another
competent mental health professional.

However, if there is no risk to the safety of your child or anyone else, the countermeasures below should serve you well.

[COUNTERMEASURES]

The countermeasures for Casting Doubt are both proactive and active. Because safety can be an issue with this Tool of
Power, we will begin with the active countermeasures.

The first and foremost concern for you as a parent is your child's safety. In Tracy's case, there is no immediate way to know if she will harm herself, but her psychiatric history is troubling. When you are uncertain, the first thing you need to do is make sure she is safe. When it comes to the three innate desires, this one always comes first. Since Tracy has threatened to harm herself, she should be taken to an emergency room to be evaluated by a psychiatric professional, who may suggest that she be admitted until her safety can be ensured. Psychologists and psychiatrists take threats of self-injury seriously, even if it may appear that the child is only seeking attention, because the possible consequences are too serious to overlook even the most tenuous threats.

The second part of your active response should be to remain consistent with your child. Listen to your child and let her know that you understand what she is saying and are aware of her concerns. And let her know what you are going to do to follow up. If your child's concerns are valid, she simply needs to know that you understand and will work as hard as you can to protect her and make things right. Empathy and action on your part to protect her are the only components needed to restore your child's sense of calm.

If you learn that your child has attempted to manipulate you by Casting Doubt, then you should sit her down and discuss the inappropriateness of her actions. Some parents will bring up the story of "The Boy Who Cried Wolf"—the prototypical story about how Casting Doubt when there is no risk reduces one's chances of getting help when one truly needs it. If you have a predetermined consequence for this type of behavior, deliver it. If not, have your child help you develop one, then enforce it. Explain to her that Casting Doubt is not an acceptable way to get her needs met.

Furthermore, stick to the limits you have set. Giving in to

your child's attempt to manipulate will only teach her that this strategy works. Let your child know that you understand her resistance to the limits you have set but that she will have to comply with your decision. You should also explain that her failure to comply might lead to punishment.

Often, children resort to Casting Doubt because they have a hard time coping with the disappointment of not getting their way. The parent's job is to help the child acquire appropriate coping skills. One of the ways children develop these skills is by learning that they can't always get what they want. Giving in to your child robs him of the opportunity to grow from that experience. Sticking to your guns may upset your child in the short term, but it will serve his best interests in the future.

The proactive way to reduce the frequency with which your child calls on this strategy is to work on reducing your *own* anxiety. Parents feel anxious for many reasons. Some worry that their child's safety or best interests are in jeopardy, while others fear that pushing their child to respect a limit that they resist will lead to unhappiness or a strained relationship between them. Regardless of the reason, there is no denying that anxious parents are confronted by Casting Doubt more often than parents who are calm and in control.

Take care of yourself and seek out support from a spouse. Enlist a psychologist to discuss parenting strategies. Share stories with other parents and friends. Doing any of these things will likely reduce your anxiety because you will discover that what you ask of your child is reasonable and what all parents expect.

Casting Doubt is often the last resort for a child who is on an emotional roller coaster. Make sure she is strapped in for the ride, but don't join her.

18

Glorification

Glorification is the strategy by which your child pleads that an object or activity is a once-in-a-lifetime opportunity, with the hope of evoking an anxious yes from you. Commonly stated: "You don't understand; it's the biggest dance of the year!" or "It's the only chance I'll get!" Regardless of the statements used, the strategy is the same: to get you to think twice before you say no.

Adam, seventeen, was an eleventh grader at a private high school. He was dating Sophia, a senior whom he would often refer to as "the hottest girl in the whole school." In our individual sessions together, Adam would focus on his anxiety over Sophia's interest in him. Adam was a star on the basketball team, had a 3.8 grade point average, and never had to worry about having friends to hang out with. He was a well-liked, popular kid. But he was filled with self-doubt, which was expressed in his obsession with Sophia's friendship with another senior boy. Because Adam and Sophia had different free periods, he was often bothered by the fact that she would choose to spend that time with the other boy. He would make statements like, "Why would she hang out with him when she's going out with me?" When I would follow up and ask him if he had asked her that question, he would respond, "No. I don't want her to think I'm insecure."

Some weeks later, Adam's school was to hold a big dance for juniors and seniors. He asked his parents for money to pay for a limousine and tuxedo, but they told him they would all be leaving town for a family gathering in Connecticut. Adam was very upset. He wanted to stay home so he could go to the dance.

In our sessions, he described horrible fantasies about how if he weren't at the dance, Sophia would spend time with the senior boy, they would kiss, and she would leave Adam. "When I see him, I'm gonna kick his ass!" Adam said of his rival. Adam wanted nothing more than to go to the dance. His anxiety was so great that it prevented him from trusting Sophia.

As a result, Adam wanted to have a family session. He felt that his parents would more likely listen to him in my office than at home.

In our meeting, Adam's parents confided that they were on the fence about letting him stay behind. They noted that they had never let him stay home alone and that they had refused to let his older sister stay home alone until she was a senior.

MOTHER: I can understand why you want to stay home. The dance is a big deal. I think your father and I need to talk. I mean, we have never left you home alone before.

ADAM: But you let Karen stay home alone for the debate retreat.

MOTHER: I know, Adam, we've talked about this. She was allowed to stay home because she was a senior. We wouldn't have let her before that.

ADAM: I know, Mom, but Karen won't care. Why don't you ask her?

MOTHER: That's not the point. If we let you stay home, it sends a message.

ADAM: What message?

MOTHER: Like we might favor you with special privileges.

ADAM: Mom, I don't want anything else. You don't understand! If I don't go, then Harrison's gonna be all over Sophia.

MOTHER: No, he's not.

ADAM: Yes, he is! Mom, you don't know. He's always trying to hang out with her. They spend free time together. They IM ["instant message"—communicate by computer or text message] each other. I mean, it's so obvious that he likes her.

MOTHER: Well, what does she think about this guy?

ADAM: I don't know. That's not the point.

MOTHER: Well, I think it is the point. If she loves you, she's not going to leave you for him.

ADAM: No, Mom. The point is, if I can't go, she will leave me and get with him.

MOTHER: Well, I don't know. What do you think? (Turns to Father.)

FATHER: I don't know. I mean, I don't think it's that big of a deal if he stays. I don't want to do anything that is gonna cause him to be this upset.

ADAM: It's just that I don't want to lose her.

FATHER: I hear that . . . loud and clear. You really think she'll break up with you if you don't go to the dance?

Adam: Yes!

You can begin to see how strongly a child can plead his case. In the end, Adam's parents let him stay behind and attend the dance.

Children who use Glorification are exploiting the empathy and anxiety of the parent. Usually parents who fall prey to this Tool of Power have a low threshold for tolerating anxiety in their child, and when they find themselves in a situation like this, they put their child's immediate happiness before his best future interests.

[COUNTERMEASURES]

To counteract Glorification, you must be fully aware of your decision-making process. Understand the importance of the object of the child's desire when you restrict him from an activity or privilege. In the example above, Adam believes that his relationship with Sophia hinges on going to the dance, an assertion that is supported by his anxious disclosures in individual therapy.

You have to weigh the consequences of your decision against the possibly negative outcome for the child. Is it wise to leave a seventeen-year-old home alone? Will he really lose the love of his life? Is it a huge exaggeration—Glorification?

Resist restricting legitimately major and meaningful events in your child's life, but don't succumb to his exaggerated claims about outcomes.

Never put your child's desires above his safety or best interests. Adam's parents were marginally worried about his safety, but they were concerned that they were affording him a privilege that wasn't offered to his sister. In the end, they gave in to his wishes and discussed the decision with the sister, who was comfortable with it.

Adam agreed to call them twice a day during the weekend and to be home in bed by 1 a.m. the night of the dance. No great harm came from their decision.

Out of insecurity, Adam had exaggerated the entire situation. He went to the dance and had less fun with Sophia than he had hoped for. He is now a senior and has a new girlfriend, and Sophia is in her freshman year at an Ivy League college.

19

Surprise Attack

A Surprise Attack is always startling and may even be funny, in the way that the old TV show *Candid Camera* was funny even while it landed the subject in an embarrassing position. When your child hits you with a plea when you least expect it, making it difficult for you to say no, she has launched a Surprise Attack.

Imagine that you are at the checkout counter of an upscale food market. As you look around, you notice that most of the people look like they just walked out of a fashion magazine. You wonder what the people ahead of you in line do for a living in order to afford that overflowing cart of gourmet foods. You wonder if you can afford the few items you place on the conveyor belt. But everyone around you seems to be happy and courteous. As he rings you up, the clerk asks, "How's your day going?" And you respond with a smile, "Great." In the midst of the pleasantries, your child decides that the time is ripe to plop down that magazine that you had already told her she couldn't have. Shocked and quite frankly stuck, you don't feel comfortable responding. After all, you don't want to make a scene or look cheap, particularly considering all those people who are looking at you. So you don't say anything. Angry inside, you just buy the magazine and choose to deal with it when you get into the car. This was a Surprise Attack: your child put you on the spot in order to improve her chances of getting what she wanted. And it worked.

[COUNTERMEASURES]

Paradoxically, the countermeasure to Surprise Attack is a reversal of the Surprise Attack. Your child counts on your discomfort to accomplish her aim, anticipating that this tool will put you on the defensive. In the example above, to give in and buy the magazine will only gratify your child and reinforce her reliance on this Tool of Power.

What your child does *not* count on is that you will be secure enough to put your foot down and risk negative reactions from the people around you. Your child has assumed that the Surprise Attack will put you in such an uncomfortable position that you will have to give in to her desires. What she has done is to project her feelings on to you. She knows that calling attention to herself would make her uncomfortable, and so she assumes that you would feel the same way. This is why she assumes this strategy will be so effective. You must prove her wrong.

It is because of the process of projection that we can feel confident that a reverse Surprise Attack will be successful. Now picture yourself back in the market. As you are checking out, your child does the unthinkable. She completely disregards your earlier refusal and plops down the magazine. Stop and think. If your child depends on your discomfort because she, too, would feel this way (projection), then it follows that drawing public attention to her would cause her considerable discomfort. Your most effective response might be to say to the clerk, "I'm sorry, sir. It seems as though my daughter is being disrespectful. I told her earlier that I would not be buying her a magazine this evening, but she must feel that by sneaking the magazine onto the checkout counter, I will change my mind and buy it." You could then turn to your child and say, "Please remove it." Most children would not want this attention. They become deeply embarrassed. I should qualify this example by saying that in my private practice, I encourage parents to avoid public embarrassment of their children. But clearly in this situation, a response like this one is reasonable and logical. The child's embarrassment is solely a product of her own misbehavior, and as such, it is okay.

In short, the countermeasure to Surprise Attack is sticking to your guns. Every parent can identify with the challenges of parenting. We often feel self-conscious in public and fear public embarrassment. This is normal. And by normal, I mean that we all feel this way at times. The fact is that when you see someone put into a situation similar to the one I just described, you might become curious, but you certainly don't become judgmental about the parent. If anything, you are empathetic because you, too, have endured the pressure caused by a misbehaving child.

About a year ago, I was working with the family of a very impulsive boy who had just turned six. The mother and father were successful businesspeople who had enrolled their children in an exclusive private school. Typically parents who place their child in such an environment cringe at the thought of the child misbehaving. This is because most of them feel that every other parent there has the perfect child. Many of the parents in schools like this are very self-conscious and feel that normal immature behavior may reflect poorly on their ability to parent as well as on how other people view their family. At a school function, this mother was speaking with another parent about an upcoming event. The two were discussing what food to bring. At this point the six-year-old boy walked up and said, "I know. You can bring poo-poo and ca-ca." His mother was horrified. And if that weren't embarrassing enough, the other parent responded by saying, "I'm so sorry for you." (I was shocked when I heard that this was her response.)

I spent weeks trying to assure this mother that every parent, including the perfect one she had been talking to, experiences situations like these. But my admonishments didn't sink in until weeks later when the "perfect" mother and her son were invited to a function at my client's home. Both mothers were wrapping presents when the other mother's son walked up laughing and said, "Mommy, I just farted on Jeffrey's head." And to seal the deal, this child farted in front of both mothers. Being the class act that my client was, she responded by saying, "Don't worry, things like this happen to all of us." Finally she had accepted the truth.

I end with this story because the countermeasure to Surprise Attack depends on your ability to stand up for what you believe is right for your child, even if you are anxious about what others may think of you at the time. Every parent will encounter situations like these, and when parents appropriately discipline their children in public, we admire them. We admire them because we know how difficult parenting can be.

Take the risk and stick to your guns.

PART THREE

DEVELOPING AN ACTION PLAN TO DECREASE PROBLEMATIC BEHAVIOR IN THE FUTURE

[20]

The Five Reasons Children Manipulate

Now that we have dispelled the three commonly held myths about parenting, we can go on to understand the five basic reasons why our children manipulate.

Given that children are good-hearted human beings who are eager to please their parents and typically feel shame and remorse when they disappoint them, why, on the other hand, are they so manipulative?

Some parents find their children's behavior so deceptive and inappropriate that they describe them as "always bad," or they say "he never listens." Such extreme descriptions are often indicative of deep relationship problems. At the root of the child's manipulation strategy is his frustration over not getting his needs met. Parents may eliminate the child's tactics of manipulation by paying attention to his underlying needs and figuring out a way to meet them. One way of accomplishing this is through the use of my Star Method of Child Temperament Assessment, which we will discuss in Chapter 21.

Children use their Tools of Power (manipulation) for five reasons:

- To obtain love, attention, and nurturance

- For self-preservation

- To bring about a self-prosperous condition

- To gain a sense of empowerment

- To even the score

Let's look at how these operate.

Love, Attention, and Nurturance

Given that our children live in a very different and some would say harsher world than many of us grew up in, it follows that they have a more obvious craving for love, attention, and nurturance.

Most adults can remember a time when only one parent worked. Today that is a rarity. With both parents working, families spend less time together.

While parents remember school fights as scary fistfights, now children may bring knives and guns to school, and we see TV news reports of school violence that makes anything most of us ever faced pale in comparison. At the time of this writing, thirty-two students had just been killed at a Virginia university.

Most parents never thought about the possibility of a war brought to American soil, yet our children are haunted by images of 9/11 and a fear of airplanes and skyscrapers beyond anything we would have ever imagined.

It's no wonder that whether out of fear, frustration, or loneliness, children resort to inappropriate behavior and manipulation to get our attention. The adage "bad attention is better than no attention at all" becomes operative in many parent-child relationships.

Our children love us. We are the most important people in their lives. And just as much as they need food, water, and shelter, they need our love, attention, and nurturance. If these needs are not met, they will turn to manipulative tools. And when those tools work, they'll turn to them again and again.

Self-Preservation

Self-preservation refers to the child's desire to avoid adverse consequences or to ensure his chances of receiving a reward. Please understand that for the purposes of this book, I am not meaning "self-preservation" in the literal sense. Rather, I am referring to a child making every attempt to increase the likelihood that he will receive something he likes or to protect something he likes from being taken away.

Self-preservation makes a lot of sense to parents because they draw on the same mechanism when relying on basic parenting strategies of rewards and punishments. However, in this case, we are talking about a child who uses his Tools of Power to allow him to perform the inappropriate behavior and to preserve the conditions in which he feels most comfortable.

A Self-Prosperous Condition

Anyone would choose fun and pleasure over disappointment. Why would children be any different?

Children find it particularly difficult to defer their immediate desires to what their parents might call "moral consciousness." Parents are often frustrated when they have caught their children lying, disobeying, or withholding information. But the frustration may really stem from misplacing logic on a child. Children's minds don't work the way adult minds work.

Failure to obtain the prize causes far more anxiety for a child than feelings of guilt for misbehavior. In fact, children are typically incapable of feeling anticipatory guilt. This is because they operate in the moment—the I-WIN mentality is in charge. Remember, guilt doesn't set in until after we act. The adult may wrongly assume that the child could have planned ahead to know that she would feel guilty. This is a misapprehension. In the moment, the child feels only a sense of anticipation, desire, or anxiety over getting what she wants.

This seeming lack of moral consciousness and behavioral control does not mean that your child will end up in jail; it just means that she is immature. As your child matures, so does her ability to control her impulses, delay gratification, and cope with the anxiety of anticipation and desire. Parents are facilitators in this process.

If we are aware of the child's I-WIN frame of mind, we can intervene without burdening the child with shame or disappointment. Laying guilt trips on a child can damage his self-esteem. Instead, a parent should address his concern over the behavior, work out a plan for solving problems when they arise, and deliver a consequence that is fair, appropriate, and logical. By remaining calm and nonjudgmental, the parent allows the child to feel free to explore alternative methods of dealing with intense feelings of excitement, desire, and anxiety.

It is worth mentioning that there are some conditions that impede the maturation process. Children with regulatory problems such as attention-deficit/hyperactivity disorder (ADHD) struggle much harder to control their impulses. Such children seem prone to acting without thinking and have great difficulty controlling frustration and disappointment. They may also need professional intervention.

Whatever the child's circumstances, parents must realize that some children use a Tool of Power (manipulation) to bring about a self-prosperous condition.

A Sense of Empowerment

Many children use their Tools of Power out of a sense of insecurity, which is evident in their continual quest to feel in control. Such children present a paradox to the outside observer. Outwardly, they seem highly confident, egocentric, and unwilling to bend from their agenda; psychologists often refer to such children as oppositional. Inside, however, these children are very insecure. And worst of all, they don't understand *why* they feel insecure.

This type of child tends to personalize most of the interactions and processes that she experiences. She places a premium on what other people say about her and how they behave toward her. As if others could do no wrong, she feels as if she herself is to blame for the world's problems. Keep in mind that on the outside, you would never know that she feels this way.

She may simply appear oppositional and irritate you. But on the inside, she thinks, "Mom's mad at me again. I always mess up," or, "Nobody cares about what I want." She never thinks, "I'm just a kid. I should never have to feel this way about myself."

In my practice, I have observed that these insecure children find it very difficult to open up and become vulnerable. When confronting their inner feelings, they are exceedingly uncomfortable and humiliated. They mask their feelings with bravado, pretending that they have no problems at all. These children are purposefully oppositional because it gives them a sense of control and empowerment. Sadly, when the brief period of time that they are allowed to feel empowered fades, they are greeted by sustained feelings of guilt, sadness, and loneliness.

As with most children, the I-WIN frame of mind is in full control. Not thinking about the sense of isolation their behavior will create, they will use their Tools of Power to gain that temporary sense of control or inner sense of self-confidence because it brings them immediate gratification during a time when they feel irritable, sad, or anxious. This immediate form of gratification far outweighs any fear that they may experience anxiety over creating distance from their parents, whom they idealize and love. It is a very sad and painful process.

Evening the Score

Operating from the given that it is a stressful world, children face the additional stress-making pressures of succeeding in school, gaining the acceptance of peers, and pleasing parents—goals that often seem to be at cross-purposes. The challenge to parents is to make the home both a safe place for children and the place where they can "let it all out."

Evening the score, as it relates to the Tools of Power, most commonly occurs as a product of anger, frustration, or disappointment. And though parents and siblings may not be the cause of the exploding emotions, they are usually the targets. Evening the score is the process by which the child vents pent-up feelings on those around him, and includes protesting when he doesn't get his way and punishing by name-calling and yelling. Evening the score involves the child acting in a way that pushes the emotional buttons of a parent and forces a reaction—most often anger. Children who manipulate to even the score are gratified by the reaction of the parent, as the reaction serves as proof that the parent is as upset as they are.

Assessing Your Child's Temperament: Using the Star Method

At this point, you may think that you have the strategies and tools that you need not only to overcome your child's attempts at manipulation but also to prevent her from manipulating in the future. After all, as I've said to parents—and to readers—again and again, *kids do what they do because it works*. And after reading Part Two, you know how to prevent the Tools of Power from being used against you. But let me pose a question that may upset your equilibrium. Why is it so wrong for your child to manipulate?

After all, who is it really hurting? Your answer might be: "Manipulation hurts me and my child. It is damaging to our relationship and creates distance between us." This is an undeniably accurate response. Manipulation eats away at the parent-child bond.

Now I don't want to dishearten you by what I am about to tell you because you have every right to feel competent in dealing with your child when she chooses to engage her Tools of Power. You've done the reading. However, there is a big qualifier to everything that has come before in this book. The interventions (countermeasures) that you have learned are all *situation specific*. That is to say, you have learned the first half of the equation—how to counteract a tool when you see it being employed—but you may be frustrated to find that your child will drag out the same tools or others in the future. Let's look at how we might set the stage for those tools to be used less frequently.

In the previous chapter, I introduced the five basic reasons that your child manipulates: (1) to obtain love, attention, and nurturance; (2) for self-preservation; (3) to bring about a self-prosperous condition; (4) to gain a sense of empowerment; and (5) to even the score. To minimize your child's use of the Tools of Power, you must be fully aware of his temperament. After all, *his temperament determines how and when he will use his Tools of Power.* For this reason, it makes sense that structuring a home environment based on the traits associated with your child's temperament will reduce his tendency to resort to his Tools of Power in the future.

Of course, determining the temperament of your child can be a very difficult task. Although a few enlightened people have an uncanny understanding of children and what they are really after—in some cases, these people are even therapists— the majority of parents report that no matter what they do, their child never seems to be content. Which brings us to

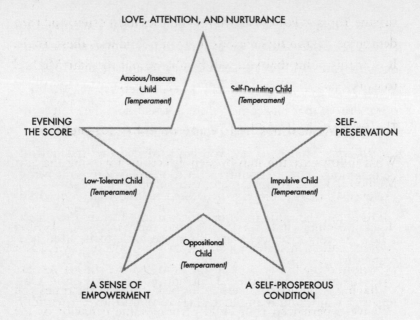

the key question: "How do I understand my child's unique temperament?"

In my practice, I have found that the temperament of a child is often revealed by the Tools of Power he employs. Underlying the Tools are the reasons why the child manipulates, and tucked within the manipulation are signs and indications that reveal the child's temperament. Through working with many children over the years, I have been able to develop a model that will allow you to turn a difficult task into something very simple. I refer to my model as the Star Method of Child Temperament Assessment.

Look at the star above. At the five points of the star, you will find the five basic reasons I have identified behind your child's need to use his Tools of Power. Your first task is to identify the Tools of Power that your child uses most often, and then determine the *top two* reasons that your child uses these Tools. It is at this point that you will be able to put the Star Method to work.

The Star Method of Child Temperament Assessment

What follows are the step-by-step directions for using the Star Method of Child Temperament Assessment:

1. Identify and circle the two reasons most frequently behind your child's misbehavior or use of her Tools of Power. You will find the five reasons at the points of the star. If you are having difficulty completing this task, think of the times you have experienced your child's troublesome behavior or the times your child has attempted to employ her Tools of Power. Then, identify the major reasons behind these tough times.

2. Once you have circled the two most frequent reasons that your child manipulates, connect the two points of the star corresponding to the circled items using the shortest distance possible as you travel around the outside of the star.

3. After completion of Step 2, locate your child's temperament(s). Your child's temperament(s) will be located in the triangle created after you connect the two points of the star. It is possible for your child to have up to two temperaments.

4. Now that you have identified your child's temperament(s), turn to the appropriate chapter(s) to learn more about his characteristics, as well as the proactive measures you can take to reduce the frequency of his manipulative behaviors.

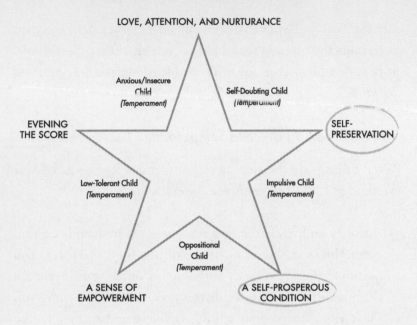

In the following example, we have identified the temperament of the Impulsive Child.

It is important to note that your child may have more than one temperament. For example, if the child uses his Tools of Power primarily for Self-Preservation and Empowerment, he would have two temperaments: Impulsive Child and Oppositional Child.

In such a case, it would be important to follow the interventions I lay out for both temperaments.

Once we have identified your child's temperament(s), we can then determine how to develop a home environment best suited to him. Because each temperament requires its own unique structure, I have provided a separate chapter for each.

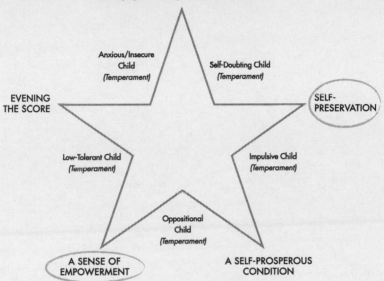

PART FOUR

SETTING STRUCTURE BASED ON YOUR CHILD'S TEMPERAMENT

Meeting Your Child's Interpersonal Needs

In this final part of the book, I will outline some customized ways to respond to the interpersonal needs of your child. Keep in mind that the interventions I discussed earlier are very important, but they are situation specific and are designed for you to respond successfully in the moment when your child employs his Tools of Power. This part aims to help you make lifestyle changes at home to reduce the need for your child to rely on his Tools of Power, or manipulative behaviors, in the future. Your child's success will depend on your adherence to the countermeasures I outlined in Part Two as well as the structural and relational changes I will lay out here, which are referred to as restrictive measures.

[22]

The Self-Doubting Child

In my experience, the Self-Doubting Child is affected by three forces: genetics, anxious parents, and an inability to feel accepted in the eyes of her peers.

In my private practice, I sometimes find myself at a loss to find environmental reasons for a child's strongly manifested insecurity. Absent environmental evidence, it seems likely that genetics play a role in severe cases of self-doubting.

We know that depression and anxiety can be genetically transmitted from one generation to the next. Such transmission is complex and not fully understood, but there is ample evidence that children who are prone to feelings of depression and anxiety are at an increased risk of falling into the category of the Self-Doubting Child.

We know that children often express very strong feelings of insecurity at an early age if their parents are habitually anxious.

Anxious parents tend to focus on life's problems rather than on positive opportunities. For a child who is exploring and experimenting, this transference of negative emotions from a parent can be acute and often leads to self doubt.

Children who grow up with anxious parents generally feel that they can never please them. Because a child typically seeks out feelings of pride derived from parental reactions, this negativity can be painfully damaging. But that's not all. It is through parents that children learn about themselves. In particular, through parental example, children learn how to resolve problems and to strive for and meet goals. Children of anxious parents learn that life is made of perpetual problems and nothing is ever good enough. And without intervention, these are themes that may carry throughout their lives.

Look at how these harmful messages affect children. Picture a child who has an interest in how a clock works. One day, when left alone, the child decides to take a clock apart. Fascinated, the child uncovers the sprockets and screws that go into making this time-telling marvel. While the child admires her handiwork, the anxious parent walks in. Mother says, "What are you doing? You broke the clock! Now it will never work right again!"

Now as any anxious parent will tell you, these verbalizations don't just stop there. They go on and on because the parent not only wants to make sure that the child heard what she said but also needs the child to validate her anxiety. So for the next ten minutes, this child will hear the same tape loop. "I can't believe you would do such a thing! What were you thinking? You broke a perfectly good clock!" Children who face such reactions often become conflict averse. They quit exploring and experimenting and learn that it is a lot safer to say something like, "I can't do it," than to risk making a mistake and igniting parental anxiety.

Anxious parents also have a knack for raising children who believe that nothing is ever good enough. If the child gets an A on a test, the anxious parent won't say, "Way to go! I knew you could do it," but may say, "Well, if you can get an A on that test, there is no good reason you can't get an A in the class, and in your other classes." Rather than validating the accomplishment, this reaction tells the child that no matter what she does, it isn't enough. It's a disincentive to succeed.

Anxious parents typically put undue pressure on young children to act more maturely than is developmentally normal. For example, a parent may reprimand her child for acting silly in the presence of adults, fearing that the other adults may be critical of her parenting skills. When children are habitually placed in such a position, they often take on what we might refer to as a "complex." They idealize the perspective of their parents and feel that if their parent sees them as silly and immature, then this is the way the world sees them.

As children move into the preteen and teen years, they retain such feelings and carry them into interactions with peers. Children who have been made to feel that they are not attractive feel insecure when put into situations with peers who place a priority on good looks. Children who are not athletic feel insecure in situations where they are judged by athletic ability. Children who feel socially insecure bring that insecurity into every relationship. And, unfortunately, these feelings may be learned in the home before the child ever goes out into the world.

Already self-doubting, such a child is reinforced in her doubt in every encounter she has with the world.

[PROACTIVE MEASURES]

If you have a Self-Doubting Child, you must work on your own anxiety and develop a stronger bond between the two of you. At the same time, you need to find a supportive peer group for your child. As we will discuss below, supportive peer groups consist of friends with similar interests, whom your child can depend on to be nice to him most of the time. In addition, seek out activities for your child in which he can gain a sense of mastery. Don't focus on his failures; help him do well at what he is good at.

One of the most difficult things to do if you're an anxious parent is to decrease your own anxiety. But you will have to do this if you want to be a more effective parent. This task cannot be achieved through simple mechanics. You must be particularly motivated. But when parents recognize how their own anxiety negatively affects their child, they are typically motivated to change.

Everyone experiences a certain amount of anxiety, and that anxiety spills into the challenging job of parenting. But if anxiety predominates your relationship with your child, you are on a dangerous course. The following are some tips that might help you avoid the dangers:

1. Have at least one friend, preferably one with children, whom you can call and talk to when you're feeling upset or anxious. Make sure that this friend isn't prone to overreacting. Don't feel that you need to depend on your spouse, because if your spouse does not share your concern, you may feel devalued and even more anxious. An understanding spouse is great, but a good friend can really help.

2. When you feel really upset or anxious, take a few minutes to process the situation before you respond. If the situation doesn't seem worthy of the intensity you are feeling, refrain from responding until you feel the intensity dissipate.

3. Attempt to figure out where your anxiety is coming from. Are you worried about what other parents may think of you? Do you fear for the safety of your child? Or are you simply a neat freak? Once you have determined the source of the anxiety, do some research. Think about how rational the thoughts behind your anxiety really are. Anxiety has a way of making us feel that the worst is inevitable.

4. If you feel that you are unable to tame your response to your anxiety, find a good therapist. Therapists are trained to help you understand the reasons for your anxiety and to help you learn ways to cope.

The Importance of Peers

All children need to feel that they are a part of a peer group, and social isolation is particularly damaging to children between the ages of nine and twenty. If you find that your child has few friends and often feels left out, do something about it. Get them plugged into a peer group in which they can feel a sense of belonging. You may, for example, contact other parents at your child's school in an attempt to get to know them better and to arrange social activities with children. The Self-Doubting Child has a very difficult time putting herself out there to ask for phone numbers or make plans. Fearing rejection, she avoids even trying.

In an attempt to avoid the pain of rejection, a child may even devalue peers and further isolate herself.

In some cases, setting up social activities involving your child may be particularly intimidating for her. You must evaluate her level of anxiety before pursuing this option.

If your attempts at finding a compatible peer group for your child fail, you may need to seek help from a child psychologist. Self-Doubting Children are often too embarrassed and humiliated to open up and be honest about the rejection they face with their peers. It may be easier for them to discuss these matters with someone who is objective.

Another way of finding a peer group is to take advantage of an activity in which your child excels. If your child is good at basketball, karate, or chess, she may also be more confident and therefore more sociable while engaging in it. Self-Doubting Children need to find a sense of mastery in a world that, for them, is always a source of doubt. Mastering a task should allow your child to excel, providing her a feeling of inner pride and, better yet, hope. These children want to feel more confident; they do not relish their inner doubt. If they can feel good about one area of their life, it allows them to feel hopeful about excelling in another.

Lastly, if you have a Self-Doubting Child, you need to work very hard at fostering a stronger connection with your child. Remember that these children may often hide things from their parents when they feel ashamed. So the shame is compounded by secrecy, which further distances the child from the parent. Empathy can go a long way toward strengthening the parent-child connection. Most parents feel compelled to fix the problem, but what the child really needs most is to know that the parent cares about her feelings. Children who seek out a parent when they are feeling hurt are approaching them from a strictly emotional level. Problem fixing works at the cognitive level, but when a child is seeking love and nurturance, resolving a problem becomes secondary. Take time to truly empathize with your child. This will strengthen her ability to soothe herself and solve her own problems in the future.

Parents can also foster a sense of connection by initiating developmentally appropriate play with their child. If your daughter is four, approach her and ask her to play a game of princesses with you. If your son is thirteen, ask him to play a video game with you. If you don't know how to play, let him teach you. And if your child is eighteen, ask him or her to go to dinner with you.

By letting go of your defenses and making your child feel like a valued part of your life, you can go a long way toward boosting his or her confidence and self-esteem.

23

The Impulsive Child: A Case of the Shuns

The Impulsive Child is often the easiest kid to spot in a crowd. Although the severity of impulsiveness may vary from child to child, this type of kid invariably struggles against delaying gratification and thinking before he acts. The most impetuous of these children are the ones who suffer from attention-deficit/hyperactivity disorder (ADHD). This is a neurological disorder defined by a group of symptoms found in the *Diagnostic and Statistical Manual-IV-TR*, the standard reference of psychological disorders used by psychologists. The following are the symptoms for ADHD,* as noted in the *DSM-IV*:

---

*It should be noted that there are three types of ADHD: Impulsive Type, Hyperactive Type, and Combined Type. The actual diagnosis of ADHD would need to be made by a professional and would be indicated by what subtype the child most closely manifests.

SYMPTOMS OF INATTENTION

1. Often fails to give close attention to details or makes careless mistakes in schoolwork, work, or other activities.

2. Often has difficulty sustaining attention in tasks or play activities.

3. Often seems not to listen when spoken to directly.

4. Often does not follow through on instructions and fails to finish schoolwork, chores, or duties in the workplace (not due to oppositional behavior or failure to understand instructions).

5. Often has difficulty organizing tasks and activities.

6. Often avoids, dislikes, or is reluctant to engage in tasks that require sustained mental effort (such as schoolwork or homework).

7. Often loses things necessary for tasks or activities (toys, school assignments, pencils, books, or tools).

8. Often is distracted by extraneous stimuli.

9. Often is forgetful in daily activities.

SYMPTOMS OF HYPERACTIVITY

1. Often fidgets with hands or feet, or squirms in seat.

2. Often leaves seat in classroom or in other situations in which remaining seated is expected.

3. Often runs about or climbs excessively in situations in which it is inappropriate (in adolescents or adults, may be limited to subjective feelings of restlessness).

4. Often has difficulty playing or engaging in leisure activities quietly.

5. Often is "on the go" or acts as if "driven by a motor."

6. Often talks excessively.

7. Often blurts out answers before questions have been completed.

8. Often has difficulty awaiting turn.

9. Often interrupts or intrudes on others (butts into conversations or games).

Keep in mind that your child may exhibit some or many of these symptoms but may not necessarily suffer from ADHD. And intensity, frequency, and multiplicity of symptoms are the keys here. A true diagnosis can be reached only after the child has been assessed by a professional. The sole purpose of presenting these symptoms here is to give you a comprehensive view of what you can expect to see from your Impulsive Child—whether clinically diagnosed as such or not.

In addition to the clinical features described above, I have come up with a more creative way to describe what afflicts the Impulsive Child: a "Case of the Shuns."

When I advise parents in my private practice that their Impulsive Child suffers from a Case of the Shuns, the response I get is usually one of concern mixed with confusion. But I quickly set them at ease as I explain that this phenomenon is to be expected when dealing with the Impulsive Child. And most important, I assure them that there is a cure.

"A Case of the Shuns" is the label I have given the Impulsive Child's typical reactions to daily life. I call these reactions "shuns" because the words that are used to describe the behaviors of the Impulsive Child end in either "-sion" or "-tion," which are pronounced "-shun." Let me explain further.

The life of the Impulsive Child can be divided into two categories: *obligations* and *passions*. Passions are those things your child loves and can't wait to do. Obligations are those things your child perceives as duties and, by definition, not fun. For example, video games may be a passion for your Impulsive Child, whereas homework is most likely an obligation. Because the Impulsive Child operates from an I-WIN (I Want It Now) frame of mind, he will always want to engage in a passion before enduring the duty of an obligation. There are two ways that a Case of the Shuns can manifest itself. The first manner is when the Impulsive Child is faced with an obligation. When this occurs, the Impulsive Child will engage in two processes: *procrastination* and *rationalization*. Without exception, the Impulsive Child will push off the obligation for as long as he can (procrastination). And he will give countless reasons and excuses about why he "should" or "could" complete the obligation later (rationalization). Parents report that their Impulsive Child may say anything in the effort to avoid having to face the stimulus that causes him displeasure. For the Impulsive Child, displeasure can simply mean that the obligation is getting in the way of a passion (something he would rather do). But regardless of the reason, an Impulsive Child will use procrastination and rationalization when faced with an obligation.

It should be noted that the Impulsive Child engages rationalization in two ways: before and after a deadline for an obligation. While procrastinating, the Impulsive Child often rationalizes that putting off an obligation is either necessary or not a big problem. As a result, the Impulsive Child usually has a great deal of difficulty in fulfilling obligations on time, and this leads directly to the second type of rationalization: excuses, reasons, and explanations why it was not his fault. Parents may hear their Impulsive Child proclaim, "But it's not my fault" or "You never told me I had to do that." These forms of rationalization become quite frustrating for parents who often report, "He'll never learn."

Let's return to the Shuns. The second way Shuns manifest themselves is when the Impulsive Child pursues a passion but is faced with having to delay gratification. Impulsive Children have a very tough time delaying gratification. The I-WIN mentality emerges as the dominant voice in the Impulsive Child's consciousness. He has to have it now. Parents often feel Steamrolled and badgered when this side of the Shuns presents itself.

Below is a diagram depicting the Shuns:

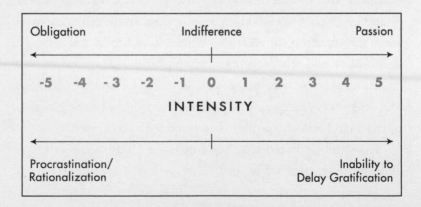

Parents are often frustrated by their Impulsive Child's Case of the Shuns and the concomitant problem of loss of motivation. These parents complain that it's like pulling teeth to get their child to engage in or complete everyday obligations such as homework or hygiene. The good news is that there is a cure for the Shuns.

[PROACTIVE MEASURES]

The proactive measures for an Impulsive Child require the following three elements:

1. A predictable structure

2. Consistent follow-through with reward and punishment

3. The cure for the Shuns (the use of contingencies)

One of the easiest ways to prevent struggles with the Impulsive Child is to *develop and maintain a predictable structure in your home*. A predictable structure means that the activities and routines in your home happen the same way every day: your child completes her homework at the same time every day, you eat dinner at the same time every evening, and you send her to bed at the same time every night. Simply speaking, you create a manageable schedule and stick to it. Without a predictable schedule, you are setting the stage for struggle and conflict.

Here's why:

The Impulsive Child has a very difficult time delaying gratification. When she knows what she wants, she becomes very anxious with anticipation and therefore tough to discourage.

Because of this deficit in her ability to cope with the anxiety of waiting, she will badger you or manipulate you until she gets what she wants. A consistent structure in the home allows your child to settle into a routine. It is this routine that will prevent her from thinking that it's an option to delay homework or stay up later than she should. Without a predictable structure, your Impulsive Child will never know if this is the day that she gets what she wants or if it is the day that you stick to what you say.

If you tell your child that bedtime is at 9:00 p.m., but in reality that time varies according to your mood or distractions of one kind or another, she will fight you endlessly to stay up later. From her perspective, she believes you should let her stay up later: "After all, last week you let me stay up until ten." Set a realistic bedtime and stick to it. Predictability keeps your child in the mode of going through the daily motions without questioning them.

On an additional note, when adults do not get what they want, they typically get disappointed. The Impulsive Child, on the other hand, will likely respond with anger and frustration. For her, there is no difference between *expectation* and *entitlement*. Because of her emotional investment, they are both the same. An unpredictable bedtime means that she *deserves* the latest of all bedtimes. And when you try to correct your inattentiveness, she may respond with something like, "You let me stay up last week until ten. Why are you punishing me and making me go to bed at nine tonight?"

Reduce the unnecessary frustration and conflict by setting a predictable schedule. You will be happier, and your child will not have to deal with the anxiety of wondering whether she will get what she wants every minute of the day.

The second proactive measure needed for the Impulsive Child is *consistent follow-through*. The rule here is very simple. Your

Impulsive Child will only believe what you say as long as your actions support your words. Any parent with an Impulsive Child knows that it takes only one time of not following through to create weeks of misery. For your Impulsive Child, your inconsistency is a sign that she has a chance at getting what she wants if she badgers you enough. If you set a limit and say no, mean it and stick to it. Words without action and idle threats don't work.

The last proactive measure that you should take is in response to the Impulsive Child's Case of the Shuns. The only real cure for the Shuns is to create motivation when none exists. This will mean using *contingencies*.

With a contingency, you make your Impulsive Child's access to the object of her desire dependent on fulfilling obligations. This idea seems very simple on a mechanical level. It requires subordinating passions to obligations. In other words, if you have a child who loves video games but resists homework, the following rule would be appropriate: Business before pleasure. Before the child ever has the chance to play her video games, she will need to complete her homework.

The cure for the Shuns requires that you structure the day in such a way that your Impulsive Child will have access to her desired goals only if she meets her obligations. Such a structure in your home will appear to have activities staggered to reflect the pattern: obligation met, reward; obligation met, reward. Although the I-WIN mentality of your Impulsive Child has led to an apparent loss of all motivation to engage in obligations, use of contingencies usually reignites the spark and brings back a little motivation where there was apparently none.

No intervention is ever fruitful without using the other two proactive measures discussed. Without drawing on all three measures, parents will likely fall prey to Tools of Power such as Steamrolling and Confrontation and Protest. But I insist that your child can learn—and your home life will become much more pleasant—if you remain calm and stick it out.

Remember that setting up household rules will establish predictability for your child and that with predictability comes expectation. With perseverance you will find that your child will expect that playing video games means getting homework done.

I should warn you that when you have an Impulsive Child, it might seem that things are getting worse before they get better. One psychologist used the example of a broken soda machine. She noted that if you go to the same soda machine every day, put your money in, press the button, and your soda comes out, the day that this doesn't happen comes as an unwelcome surprise. Most people don't just say, "That's odd," and walk away. One is more likely to curse, push the change return, press all the buttons, and—depending on the frustration level—even shake or kick the machine. This is likely to happen in your interactions with your child.

The Impulsive Child has had things the same way for most of her life. She isn't going to just shrug her shoulders and walk away when you change the rules of the game. She is going to shake the soda machine and make sure that you really mean what you say. Stand your ground, because if you make it past this point, your child will begin to incorporate these new rules as an expectation, just as you would begrudgingly but finally give up on that soda.

For those parents who are still having a difficult time with their child despite the interventions I have suggested, my advice is to seek professional help from a qualified child psychologist. It will help your child learn and grow, and she will even thank you for it later.

24

The Oppositional Child

When using my Star Method of Child Temperament Assessment, you will notice the term "Oppositional Child." This child displays the symptoms of the diagnosis oppositional defiant disorder. The following are the key clinical features relevant to these children, as listed in the *DSM-IV*:

1. Often loses temper.

2. Often argues with adults.

3. Often actively defies or refuses to comply with adults' requests or rules.

4. Often deliberately annoys people.

5. Often blames others for own mistakes or misbehavior.

6. Often is touchy or easily annoyed by others.

7. Often is angry and resentful.

8. Often is spiteful or vindictive.

The Oppositional Child seems perpetually irritated and annoyed. He has little tolerance for the imperfections of others and even less tolerance for rules and boundaries and those who enforce them. These children contest everything that gets in the way of their control. Many parents of Oppositional Children report that it seems as though their child is always looking for an argument. This symptom alone is enough to bring any parent to the brink of exhaustion, but to compound the conflict, parents will say that no matter how much they try to connect with the child, they are pushed away.

The Oppositional Child often loses his temper. He carries a chip on his shoulder and tends to strike out at those around him. He will either protest overtly or use passive aggression to push the emotional buttons of those with whom he is irritated. As any parent of an Oppositional Child will tell you, these children can raise quite a protest. If your child simply yells at you, consider yourself fortunate. Some of these children are physically aggressive and even violent (clear signs that professional intervention is called for). Despite the volatility of the Oppositional Child, some of these children find emotional button pushing much more gratifying and cathartic than acting out. Such children prefer to light the fuse of their target, sit back, and watch the fireworks. Many of these children find anger and irritability in others amusing as well as gratifying. Parents who endure the intensity of anger and frustration that these children provoke and who have also witnessed their children laughing at them will sometimes act out in ways that are regrettable. I have seen parents react by hitting their children, withholding food, and locking them out of the house in cold weather. These are the wrong solutions and a sure sign that the family needs professional help.

Perhaps the only way to get the Oppositional Child to say "black" is to say "white"—what used to be called in lay terms "reverse psychology." Often parents will say that their child simply disagrees for the sake of disagreeing. This predictability can be used to a parent's advantage when these children are younger. For example, if they want their child to wear a coat, they might say something like, "I don't think you need to wear your coat." Such ploys are not healthy in the long run, but many parents find themselves using them because they work in the moment. I say that they are unhealthy tactics because they feed in to the oppositional nature of the child. I also believe that you should always be honest and consistent with your child. Reverse psychology can leave a child distrustful and suspicious, increasing his oppositional behavior as he gets older.

As the Oppositional Child grows, he tends to become less predictable because he learns to mask his feelings. He typically becomes more guarded, and almost instinctively acts in opposition to the way you would like him to act. He can't bear to think that he has relinquished control to you. If you have such a child, you know how difficult it is to cope with the constant opposition and struggle for control.

In addition to the constant clashes with others, the Oppositional Child avoids accepting responsibility for his mistakes. To others, it may appear that the Oppositional Child thinks he can do no wrong because he is capable of justifying anything. And it is this additional trait in a series of others that often leads parents to want to just give up.

The last characteristic of the Oppositional Child is his ability to remember inequities and the perceived wrongdoings of others. Such children have a propensity for seeing themselves as victims and seeking revenge against those whom they perceive as having assaulted them. It is hard for them to let go and forget. They typically appear irritated and annoyed and seem to seek out conflict.

You need professional help if you are raising an Oppositional Child. You can attempt to use the countermeasures I have laid out in earlier chapters, and you can make the changes I am about to suggest, but be aware that the Oppositional Child is the most difficult child to raise. If you have an Oppositional Child, you and your family are at heightened risk for anxiety, physical abuse, divorce, and substance abuse. I strongly suggest professional intervention for families living with an Oppositional Child.

Parents of such children will find it nearly impossible to get them to do the simplest things. Often, they find that their children show them no respect and rarely follow directions. The parent-child roles have broken down. And for parents of those children, the situation can seem hopeless. Fortunately, there is help.

[PROACTIVE MEASURES]

Although the Oppositional Child is one of the toughest parenting challenges, there are things you can do to decrease the frequency with which you will be subjected to your child's use of the Tools of Power. Below is a list of the proactive measures I recommend:

1. Choose your battles wisely.

2. Always avoid power struggles.

3. Develop your ability to appear calm when faced with frustration.

4. Develop and maintain a consistent environment.

5. Develop your ability to predict difficult times and situations for your child.

6. Develop plans to deal with inappropriate behaviors before your child engages in them (post these plans in the home).

7. Work on changing only one or two behaviors at a time.

8. Use responsibilities to reward your child.

9. Seek out social support.

10. Take time off from parenting.

When dealing with an Oppositional Child, you must understand that *any* situation can become a crisis. There doesn't have to be a rational reason. Many parents that I work with make statements like, "I don't know what happened. First he said he wanted to go to his friend's house, and then he said he wanted to have his friend come here. I told him he needed to make up his mind, and he blew up." The Oppositional Child tells you a lot about how he is feeling through his behavior. The problem is that you don't get any warning—you only get the chaos. In the case of waffling over going to the friend's or having the friend over, the child became angry because he couldn't make up his mind, but he didn't want to be pressured to make a decision. Those closest to him paid a price. In this case, as in many others, the Oppositional Child attempts to pull others into the conflict so that he can cathartically act out. Of course, any parent who chooses her battles wisely would have to walk away from this one.

Choosing your battles wisely requires a few basic conditions on your part. First, you need to be secure enough in yourself that you don't need your child's validation that you are the one in charge or that he did something wrong. If you lack this security, you will be in for a world of hurt. The Oppositional Child preys on such parents because they are so easy to punish. The key to understanding your power in the relationship is to understand that the only power your Oppositional Child has is to push your emotional buttons. Think about it. What else can he do? You have all the money. You most likely drive him everywhere or pay for the car he uses. And you are the one who is there to clean up the mess when he really needs you to. Maintaining this perspective can shield you from your child's power play. And you must always walk away from your child's attempt to pull you into a power struggle.

Second, choosing your battles wisely depends on appreciating the fact that the environment can often work to your advantage. In the case of the child who cannot make up his mind regarding the location of his playdate, the prompt by his parent led to an outburst. As many parents would tell you, there probably wasn't much this parent could have said to decrease the child's frustration. Even if the parent had places to go and things to do, putting pressure on the child would only have made matters worse. The parent could have said, "Well, just let me know when you have made up your mind," and gone about her business. Walking away ends the power struggle. And the child is left with the delayed gratification of a playdate until he can make up his mind.

At this point you may be thinking, "He sure makes it sound

easy. But what if my son follows me around the house and doesn't let it go?" And that is a realistic possibility.

Oppositional Children persist in interacting in order to establish control. They need to have all the answers, and when they don't get them, they need a distraction. A power struggle or fight with a parent often serves as the perfect distraction. And for many of them, getting under the skin of a parent is gratifying not only because it gives them the sense of control they are looking for but also because it allows them to cathartically dump all the frustration they are carrying inside.

It fills a need for the Oppositional Child to make others frustrated or upset when he feels frustrated. Don't fall for it. He is employing the Tools of Power that I refer to as Punishment and Tactical Engagement. To respond will only strengthen your child's dependency on these strategies in the future. As difficult as it may seem, remain stoic and allow the environment to do the work for you. If you are calm and deliver a consequence when called for, you will have gained an edge. And over time, these little victories will lead to bigger change in the child's behavior.

One of the best strategies I have discovered for dealing with an Oppositional Child is to rely on his impulsiveness. Because the Oppositional Child likes things a particular way and because he often responds as a creature of habit, maintaining a consistent structure in the environment can reduce the power struggles that may arise throughout the day. Similar to the approach with an Impulsive Child, you must place obligations above passions. If you can devise an itinerary for the day and adhere to it consistently, you may find that your child will take for granted certain things that would usually bring about a power struggle.

Focusing on homework is a perfect example. Many parents in my practice have decided to structure homework so that it starts as soon as the child comes home from school. In addition, the child is told that playtime or television and computer game time will begin only after the completion of homework. If this is a new routine, most parents face an outburst of protest. But many find that after the protest ends, their child adjusts and does his homework as scheduled. Also, these parents gain the benefit of leverage. Any resistance to doing homework is met with the standard line, "If you need help, just let me know. I'm not forcing you to do your work, but no TV or game time until it is finished." This leverage allows parents to remain firm and allow the environment to do the work for them, diminishing the need to fight over homework.

So remember, always sticking to a contingency-based structure at home allows you, the parent, to enjoy some leverage for a change. And remaining consistent increases the chance that your Oppositional Child may simply do what you need him to do without question.

Predicting your child's cycles or typical reactions in given situations also proves beneficial when raising an Oppositional Child. Planning ahead for tough situations will enable you to respond calmly and with integrity (ensuring your ability to parent in the best way possible). Remaining calm and consistent is far more difficult when you are caught off guard. Planning ahead can also allow you to make the necessary changes in the environment to avoid any anticipated bumps in the road. If you are a mother who is constantly harried when trying to get your child somewhere on the weekend, you may choose to have your husband trade off with you. Or if you know that your child always fights when leaving his friend's house and you are pressed for time because you have to make an appointment, you may arrive at the friend's house a little earlier to give yourself enough time to get through the struggle and still make your appointment. Having thought through these situations in advance allows you to avoid much of the unnecessary stress, making it easier to remain calm.

Forethought can also prove valuable in the delivery of consequences to your child. Many parents find that it is very difficult to remain consistent with an Oppositional Child because they find themselves flying by the seat of their pants. And because their child brings out the worst in them, they tend to overreact or deliver consequences that they cannot enforce. The Oppositional Child is very quick to pick up on and exploit these situations. If he knows you will not be consistent, he gains confidence that he can push a little harder and still avoid a serious consequence. Planning consequences in advance will make enforcement easier. Post consequences for inappropriate behavior on the wall like an edict, so that your child is fully aware that Action A equals Consequence B. Perhaps the greatest benefit of planning is that you gain greater control while maintaining integrity in your relationship with your child.

Keep in mind, too, that you should never focus on more than two behaviors at once. Be patient. If you are always focusing on the behavior of the day, your child will feel overwhelmed and criticized. Instead, have a talk with your child. Tell him the one or two behaviors that you are going to be focusing on, and do just that. Praise your child for doing well and avoid focusing on other behaviors. When you find that your child has progressed to the point in which he is 80 to 90 percent responsive in those areas, have another meeting with him, reward him, and allow him to graduate from those behavioral goals and then bring in a new behavior as you leave off on the last. If you have an Oppositional Child, understand that you may be provoking your child if you expect too much. Minimize the behaviors you focus on at one time; otherwise, you will come across to your child as hypercritical.

Be specific. Rather than saying, "We're working on your being more respectful," say, "We are working on your not saying the F word." Parents in my practice who have failed to focus on specific goals admit that their children are slow to change. Also, their children see them as unduly harsh. When an Oppositional Child views his parents as overly harsh, he acts out more. So be specific, stay focused, be consistent, and use responsibility as a tool.

Here is a lesson from theories of organizational psychology. If one is unhappy with his job, paying him more doesn't lead to greater job satisfaction. Rather, job satisfaction grows most when one is given more power to make changes and control his environment. Organizational psychologists refer to this additional power as "responsibility." When I was in fifth grade, my teacher, Ms. Goodlett, once asked if anyone wanted to clean her erasers. Nearly every hand shot up. It seems laughable that everyone was eager to choke on chalk dust, but why were we so eager? We were eager because it was a privilege. It was a responsibility. And it was a responsibility because she made us "earn the privilege."

The Oppositional Child wants to have that control and power. He wants to make choices and engage in activities that affect other people.

As a parent, your job is to figure out what responsibilities your child would want to earn and allow him to earn them. Maybe it involves choosing and helping in the preparation of dinner. Or maybe it's picking a movie or game for the family to play. Remember: Responsibility *equals* reward.

Up until this point, we have focused on proactive measures you can directly apply to your child. But I would like to switch gears and focus on you, the parent. After all, you need to take care of yourself in order to take care of your Oppositional Child.

Seeking out social support and taking time off from parenting are very effective ways of recharging your batteries and reducing the toxic impact of stress. A recent journal study focused on men who gave up their job to stay at home and women who left home to enter the workforce. The results indicated that the health of the men in the study became substantially worse after they gave up their jobs, while the women thrived after they entered the workforce. What could explain this reversal? What had the men lost and the women gained? The answer in the study: social interaction. Social interaction is a clear antidote to stress. Further research indicates that a strong social network significantly lowers the risk of depression.

Parents who have an Oppositional Child usually suffer higher levels of stress and anxiety. Therefore, it is profoundly important that such parents seek out activities and relationships to counteract stress. Unfortunately, they tend to do just the opposite.

Many such parents fail to seek out the support they need because they fear other parents may criticize their parenting. After all, they have so many problems with their children—as if no one else does. In my practice, these parents often report that they have "no time" to interact with friends and other supporters. They are just too busy. Beware: Avoiding social interaction puts you at a much higher risk both for health problems and for relationship problems with your spouse, child, and peers. Isolation also increases the likelihood that you will fall prey to depression and anxiety, and may even lead to child abuse. Why would you want to increase your burden? Make time to see your friends. If necessary, write it into your schedule. Talk to other parents about the problems you are having. Believe it or not, they most likely have parenting problems as well. I know this because I see them in my office. And trust me when I say that they will appreciate your honesty and thank you for allowing them to vent as well.

The last bit of advice I want to give you is to take a vacation. Find someone to watch the kids and head out of town. So many parents fight with one another when they have an Oppositional Child. It is sad, but I am often told something like, "We got along so well before we had children." After the children, their sex lives ended, as did the commitment to teamwork.

While children can bring out the best in couples, they can also draw out the worst. You must make time for you and your spouse to be alone together and to get back in touch with the love that brought you together. Mark vacation times (without the kids) on your calendar. If you haven't done so, do it right now. Pay attention to your needs and to the needs of your spouse and take care of yourselves. I guarantee you will be better parents.

Granted, the Oppositional Child is a difficult challenge. Try some of the solutions above, but if they don't work, don't despair. It may be beyond your immediate skills. If so, get help from an expert in oppositional defiant disorder. And don't ever forget that Rule 1 in child rearing is to first take care of yourself and your spouse.

25

The Low-Tolerant Child:
A Need for Control

The Low-Tolerant Child presents a complex picture to a parent. This child shows a fragility in her difficulty in coping with changes in the environment, but she can also be headstrong and rebel when the environment doesn't meet her needs. She can be extraordinarily manipulative. Parents with such children talk of their child's obsession with controlling her environment.

The Low-Tolerant Child:

1. Has a tremendous need to be in control.

2. Shows confidence on the outside but is really insecure on the inside.

3. Is anxious when faced with change or transition.

4. Has an extremely heightened sense of expectation and anticipation.

5. Has strong feelings of entitlement.

6. Is easily disappointed, upset, or angered.

7. Has a heightened aversion to frustration.

8. Lashes out to punish others when her needs are not met.

9. Often feels that the environment or authority figures are unfair.

10. Overpowers her caregiver emotionally, physically, or both.

11. Knows how to exploit the emotions of others.

Whether it is moving to a new home, changing schools, or deciding on a restaurant, the Low-Tolerant Child claims an emotional stake in every situation and is both resistant to change and intent on affecting the outcome of decisions that should rest in the hands of adults. They crave predictability. Some parents describe this as entitlement, but it is accompanied by a struggle over change. Every change in the environment may be perceived as a threat.

You may suggest going out for Chinese food but then change it to pizza. The anxiety lever is switched on because the Low-Tolerant Child was set on Chinese. So, to even the score, she lashes out against the parent. She may even prefer pizza, but what is really at stake is that her expectation has been thwarted. So she lashes out at her parents, calling them "liars" and refusing to eat. The sad thing is that the true reason for the child's anxiety is never articulated, and the parents never really know the root of the problem.

Below the surface, the Low-Tolerant Child might have fantasized about what she would have ordered at the Chinese restaurant, subliminally savoring the taste of the sweet-and-sour pork.

While it is normal to feel disappointment, in this case expectation has turned into entitlement, which is thwarted by the parents' change of plans. Change equals threat. A change in plans usually leads the Low-Tolerant Child to feel undervalued, not considered, or cheated. It is common for these children to make statements like, "You never listen to me" or "You just don't care about what I want." Remember the I-WIN mentality (I Want It Now) and you will recall that "coping" or "compromise" is not in this child's vocabulary. But in addition to having to cope with the loss of her expectation, your Low-Tolerant Child will need to give the new idea of pizza a chance. And for her, this only causes more agitation. After all, she doesn't want pizza! She wants Chinese food!

To better illustrate this sense of entitlement and disappointment on an adult level, there is an analogy that I often use with parents in my practice. Imagine that a Mercedes-Benz dealership calls and tells you that you have just won a contest that enables you to pick any car you want off the lot. With excited anticipation, you head right over. But halfway there, your cell phone rings and the formerly upbeat voice tells you, "We are very sorry, but it seems that we made a mistake. You are not the winner after all but the runner-up. Sorry for the inconvenience." You are exasperated and disappointed. An hour later, now back at home, you get another call. This time the voice tells you, "We're really sorry about our mistake and have decided to give you a new bicycle, which is worth six hundred dollars. Again, we are truly sorry." This is the type of good news that would make anyone happy. They are giving you a valuable new bicycle. But it is still a disappointment because of the adrenalin rush over anticipating a new car. You have just come down from a stomach-churning roller-coaster ride.

The Low-Tolerant Child is on this ride almost daily, even though the parent may consider the child's concerns trivial. The intensity of emotion often trumps the importance of the trigger-ing incident. Immaturity and lack of coping skills turn missing a Chinese meal into a disappointment felt as intensely as your losing a Mercedes.

Parents of Low-Tolerant Children are often perplexed when I tell them that their children are plagued by insecurity. But as we explore the difficulty these children have in admitting to or tak-ing responsibility for their mistakes, it begins to become clearer. These children often shut down or throw a tantrum before admit-ting to others that they are wrong. They fear that if they make a mistake, others will judge them severely and consider them inca-pable. Only by avoiding mistakes can they avoid public embar-rassment and maintain confidence in relation to others. After all, if those around them lack confidence in them, they might ques-tion the Low-Tolerant Child's greatest insecurity: whether or not they really do know what they are talking about.

These children fear that if they are found out, no one will listen to them or value what they have to say. We all doubt our-selves at times and lack confidence in how others perceive us, but the Low-Tolerant Child fixates on these feelings.

Another manifestation of this insecurity is that these children are overly protective of friends and caregivers. They become hostile toward anyone who, in their belief, poses a threat to their relationship with those to whom they feel close. In my practice, I have listened to countless stories of parents whose Low-Tolerant Children have physically attacked siblings and peers. In some cases, a parent can even be the target. Sometimes it is over the perception that a sibling is getting too much attention. I've been told of a child who threw rocks at other children on the school grounds out of jealousy over a friend. A child has told a parent coming home from work to go away because that parent was threatening his time with the other parent. These children are insecure at a deep level, but their intense quest for control is often manifest as a façade of confidence that leaves parents falsely believing that they have the utmost self-assurance.

Perhaps the most frustrating aspect of Low-Tolerant Children is their savvy ability to wage psychological warfare against those closest to them. They have an uncanny strength and ability to push the emotional buttons of those around them, while often making themselves appear as victims.

Gina, a Low-Tolerant Child, wants a cookie before dinner. She approaches her mother and says, "I want a cookie." Her mother appropriately responds, "Not now, sweetheart. We're about to have dinner." But Gina feels that she should have the cookie anyway. Any logic suggesting that she will not eat her dinner after having the cookie seems ludicrous. So she asks again, "But, Mom, I want a cookie now." Only this time, she starts to whine and pout as she pushes Mom's sensitive "I love you, I'll do anything for you" button. But Mom's not falling for it. She responds, "Look, it's almost time for dinner. Eat your dinner first and then you can have a cookie." Gina says, with her whine turning to a shout, "But, Mom, I don't want dinner; I want a cookie." Mom replies firmly, "Look, you're not going to have a cookie, and that's final."

This angers Gina, but does she throw a tantrum? Maybe she does, but like many Low-Tolerant Children, Gina is more gratified by the position, "If I have to feel miserable, then you have to feel miserable, too." And so the battle is waged. Gina knows by the change in her tone that Mom is getting upset at her continuing plea. She also concludes that she is not going to get the cookie and that since she has to suffer, so should Mom. Therefore, she persists. However, her intention has shifted from the desire to get the treat to the desire to get back at Mom. "All right, Mom, how about you let me have half of a cookie?" she asks. Mom (whose anger is rising) states in an ever-firmer voice, "You really need to stop asking me or else you're not even going to have one after dinner." But Gina doesn't care. She is gratified by the escalating intensity of Mom's responses. "But, Mom, just one bite," Gina adds, prompting Mom to yell, "How many times do I have to tell you? Just knock it off! You're not getting a cookie!" Remember, Gina has already accepted the loss of the treat and as a result feels angry at Mom. She wants Mom to feel miserable as well. Therefore, Mom's anger gratifies Gina. It makes her feel as if things are even now. And this is precisely what happens when Low-Tolerant Children don't get their way.

Keep in mind that this is only one example of how the Low-Tolerant Child pushes buttons. Although this Tool of Power looks like Steamrolling, it is, in fact, Punishment. Depending on the parent's vulnerability, these children may use profanity, tantrums, name-calling, and even physical assault.

Low-Tolerant Children are masters at manipulating the emotions of others to their advantage. They can sense when parents have worn down, and they exploit their exasperation, taking advantage of any weakness or insecurity. Be on guard.

[PROACTIVE MEASURES]

The Low-Tolerant Child pushes the buttons of a parent in order to seek revenge for a perceived injustice. These children will often react to limits with tantrums and meltdowns, with parents all too often capitulating by letting go of the limits out of fear of the child's emotional reaction. As a result, the child is rewarded for bad behavior. He tells himself, "If I make a strong enough protest for a long enough time, my parents will break down and give in."

In this kind of family dynamic, I am often told by parents that the child responds very differently to each of them. But the child's response depends on the parent's behavior. Often, one parent identifies with the emotional struggle of the child, whereas the other parent thinks the child has a behavioral problem that warrants stronger limits and boundaries. In these cases, I tell the parents to try switching roles. If Mom is hassled by her son every morning, I put Dad in charge of getting him ready for school. If Dad doesn't experience the same grief as Mom did, it is probably because he has a history of having set clear boundaries that the son won't breach. Such an experiment can tell you a lot about your parental management style.

There are two reasons why you never want to engage in psychological combat with your child. First, children have much more stamina and will simply outlast you, and second, the Low-Tolerant Child is simply better at the game than you are.

How might a parent meet the interpersonal needs of the child and diminish his use of the Tools of Power? Stick to the following path, and you will go a long way toward creating a stabler family dynamic.

1. Stay calm when at all possible.

2. Maintain consistent rituals at home for bedtime, dinnertime, and getting started for the day.

3. Choose battles wisely.

4. Allow for times when your child can exert control.

5. Stay away from the center of a tantrum so that the child is not fortified by your emotional reaction.

6. Allow the Low-Tolerant Child to earn responsibilities.

7. Give the Low-Tolerant Child perks.

8. Reward the Low-Tolerant Child for appropriate responses.

9. Arrange for and encourage the child to spend time with friends, and when possible, act as a social coach.

10. Provide special time to foster a stronger sense of family connection.

Maintain your poise. It's obviously hard to do if you find yourself in the middle of a whirlwind, but it is of the utmost importance. Any emotional charge coming from you will be exploited by your child. Think about it. If you get angry and your child's goal is to make you angry, you've been exploited. If you back off when your child attempts to make you feel sad or doubtful because you have set a limit, you've been exploited. You won't always know that your child is manipulating your emotions. These children are very crafty. But you can remain consistent by staying poised.

Consistency and predictability—routines—are the keys to

living with a Low-Tolerant Child. If the routine is that home-work is completed before video games are played, children do their homework without question. On the other hand, parents who vacillate with the moods of their child find themselves at the center of the chaos. Rituals can trump chaos. In my practice, I often suggest that parents write down routines and post them on walls or the refrigerator. That makes them official.

Of course, even if you do all you can to set up consistency, there will still be battles to be fought. But you can reduce them over time. Paradoxically, although the Low-Tolerant Child will fight boundaries, he also wants to know where the lines are drawn. This child struggles with chronic anxiety, and that anxiety is softened in direct proportion to the predictability of the environment. Deep down these children are unsure of their decision making, and they fear making mistakes. You dampen this fear, and gain their confidence, when you set the structure. They, in turn, gain a sense of safety knowing that if they find themselves in a mess, you will be there to help them clean it up. Anger over limits and boundaries is, as counterintuitive as it may seem, a signal of the safety they feel. Think about it. Some people displace their anger onto a family pet for the sole reason that they know they will be safe. The family pet will not kill them. They don't take their anger out on the scary pit bull down the street. If your Low-Tolerant Child lashes out in anger, it means he feels safe enough in his environment to do so.

As a rule of thumb, when your child throws a tantrum, you should give him space. Psychologists refer to tantrums as the peak of a crisis. And as any good psychologist will tell you, nothing is ever resolved while a child is in crisis. The Low-Tolerant Child presents an even more complex picture for a parent because when she approaches him while he is in crisis, she is set-ting herself up to be exploited. Here's how it works: You seek to comfort him when he is upset, but he responds to your soothing by making a demand on you or acting out to even the score. So remember, when your child is in crisis, give him space until he calms down. The only exception to this rule is when your prop-erty is being destroyed or your child's safety is endangered.

Also, use external circumstances to your advantage. For example, many parents with Low-Tolerant Children complain that when it is cold outside, they have to fight to get their child to wear a coat. Why not avoid the power struggle? Try this approach: "Look, I really don't want to argue with you. I am suggesting that it is cold outside and you may want to wear a coat. If you think that's a bad idea, do what you think is right." By responding with a statement like this, parents avoid a power struggle. Then if the child chooses to leave home without a jacket and gets cold, he suffers the consequences of his own decision. In the end, the child will be thankful for his parent's insight, especially when that parent has planned ahead and kept an extra jacket in the car.

This is a clear case of "cleaning up the mess." In such a situ-ation, the parent takes her time getting the coat out of the car so that the experience registers with the child. Let him feel a little discomfort before making him comfortable. This is where the learning occurs. But be smart about choosing your battles. If a child is late for school, don't write him an excuse (you aren't the one who is late). Let him receive the tardy mark or serve detention. If your child refuses to eat, let him. He will be hungry later. You aren't his guardian angel; you are the parent. By let-ting him bear responsibility for his actions, your life together will become less of a power struggle and more of a collaborative effort.

As for giving the child occasions to feel in control, these children, like everyone, need to feel important and valued. If your child has responded appropriately or behaved well, tell him that you are proud of him and give him a chance to call the shots. Perhaps he can decide where the family will go to dinner or what movie you will rent. If you play board games, let your child choose the game. Or allow your child to pick out her new clothes for school. Of course, these choices will have to be within acceptable limits and are not blanket endorsements. They should be occasional and directly connected with good behavior. After all, good behavior demonstrates a child's ability to make good choices and to handle responsibility. And as counterintuitive as it may seem, giving these children incrementally more control actually reduces their need for control in the future.

Let's take a closer look at how a Low-Tolerant Child attempts to cope with insecurity through maneuvering for control. Think about the five most valuable possessions you own. They may have monetary value or high sentimental value to you. Once you have thought of these five objects, imagine yourself in a kindergarten classroom with thirty five-year-old children. Your five most valuable possessions are set around the room for these children to play with. As you watch this happen, my guess is that you will feel anxious. As one child picks up your late mother's necklace, you may yell, "Wait! Don't play with that! You're going to break it!" You are understandably anxious. How might you reduce this anxiety? The obvious solution is to collect your possessions and secure them in a safe place. And by doing this, you are exerting control. Think about this. In order to feel less anxious, you need to take control. Clearly, there is comfort in control. By controlling the environment, you quickly reduce anxiety.

Operating from the I-WIN mentality, the Low-Tolerant Child is in a perpetual struggle for a sense of control and empowerment. She, like you in the scene where your mother's jewelry is handled recklessly, seeks comfort through control. Most parents who understand this concept ask, "What can we do to help comfort our children so that they don't have such a need for control?" I answer with some of the following suggestions.

Low-Tolerant Children thrive by being given responsibilities around the home. These responsibilities are privileges rather than chores and allow children to help or to make choices that affect others around them. It has to do with framing. Take the case of my fifth-grade teacher asking us to clean her erasers. By framing it as a privilege and restricting it to students who exhibit good behavior, every child in the class is eager to take on what might otherwise seem to be a thankless task. In the home, you might tell your Low-Tolerant Child that you feel she is mature enough to help cook dinner. By letting her know she has to earn this privilege, you set an example and a goal for the other children.

Closely related to responsibilities are perks. Perks are privileges that accrue to the child in relation to his position of importance in the family. Perks are inherited through a child's role as big sister or younger bother. Being the big sister, your Low-Tolerant Child may get to say grace at the dinner table three out of four nights. Being the younger brother, your child may get to have a special "younger brother" book read to him at night before bed. Or being the older brother, your child may get to stay up thirty minutes later than his younger sibling. Perks, unlike responsibilities, are never taken away.

In addition to valuing perks, the Low-Tolerant Child enjoys being rewarded for appropriate behavior. And one of the most effective rewards is money. In my practice, I give parents what I call "Proud Dollars." Proud Dollars are basically play money that I create on a computer. Along with a printed monetary value, they carry a statement like, "I Am Proud of Myself" or "Great Job!"

Parents are urged to write an accomplishment of their child's on the Proud Dollar and to sign it. After they have done this, they give the Proud Dollar to their child who, in turn, can place it in her "bank." The bank is a see-through plastic container that is kept in a visible place, such as on top of the refrigerator. At the end of the week, I encourage families to go on a Proud Dollar run where they can spend their accumulated Proud Dollars, which you convert into the real thing. (When the child uses a Proud Dollar, a hole is punched into it and it is returned to the child so that she can reread all the wonderful things she has done.) The Low-Tolerant Child gains a sense of empowerment from the ability to walk into a store and have complete control over what she will do with the money she has earned. Sometimes the child will defer gratification, saving the money until she has earned enough to buy a big-ticket item— giving her another chance to make a decision.

The final task in meeting the interpersonal needs of the Low-Tolerant Child is to help her make relationships work successfully. While some of these children can do well socially, others struggle to find a single friend. For those who do well, you may find that they are perpetually anxious over having the trendiest clothes or other material items that they equate with fitting in socially. This is a problem of its own, but for others, the greater problem is making friends at all or focusing too much energy on one friend.

On the plus side, unlike with the Oppositional Child, these children will typically confide in their parents. They are capable of discussing their socializing problems. You must assure them that you love them and point out that they have the strengths required to forge friendships. Sharing applicable experiences with your child can also be reassuring. For example, you might confide in him that "when I was seven, I felt like nobody in my class liked me. I was sure of it. So I was mean to the other kids. I remember I had a friend named Billy, and I wouldn't let anyone else play with him. I was afraid they would take him from me. Billy didn't like me controlling him, and after a while, he didn't want to play with me. I only started to have more friends when I tried to ignore my worries about people not liking me and tried to play with the other kids. After that, Billy wanted to play with me again." If your child knows he's not alone with his problem, it becomes easier for the two of you to work it out.

After this level of comfort is achieved, you can then make a very specific and concrete list of the traits your child possesses that get in the way of his making and keeping friends. You can then work on them one at a time.

I run social skills groups in which I define the difference between social rules and social fluency. An example of a social rule is that one should not burp out loud. Social fluency refers to one's ability to interact and apply social rules fluently. I once took a group to a bowling alley to work on social fluency. During the activity, one of the boys in the group let out a loud burp. This was a violation of a social rule. But just afterward, another boy in the group burped as well, and the two laughed and bonded. Although this is clearly a violation of a social rule, in a crude way it demonstrates social fluency. Social fluency can only be learned through experience. Low-Tolerant Children usually possess a detailed knowledge of social rules. Social fluency is the main area in which they struggle and need practice.

One of the most effective ways that I have found to establish fluency is through the use of inconspicuous passwords. You and your child determine passwords that will prompt your child to work on a specific goal while playing with a friend. For example, if your child is working on being fair, you may choose the password "glasses." When only you and your child know the password, your child can be prompted without being embarrassed. Armed with the password, you may arrange a playdate for your child. Ideally she can help in this process. During the playdate, you supervise your child's ability to play fair. When she stumbles, you say something like, "Have you seen my glasses?" Your child is prompted by the password and works to play more fairly. If she isn't responsive to your password, you can call her aside to talk about how she can work toward her goal. This process has proven very successful in my practice. Experiential work like this provides the best lessons in social fluency.

When working on the Low-Tolerant Child's relationship with her parents, the situation is quite different because these children are aware of their tendency to push buttons, and they usually feel bad after doing so. This sense of guilt or remorse can be projected onto parents, leading the child to fear her parents don't like her. This can be exacerbated by parental reactions.

Parents of the Low-Tolerant Child need to find time to work on fostering a closer attachment to their child. The three most powerful ways to do this are (1) involving your child in activities in which she can educate you, (2) responding to her emotional needs when she is in pain, and (3) watching videos or looking at pictures of her when she was a baby or toddler.

Remember that these children *love to be in control*. I know that if you're a parent of a Low-Tolerant Child, this is one thing you will never forget. But put this aside and give her a chance to have control when it is appropriate and you can both enjoy yourselves. Let her educate you. If she wants to play a video game with you, let her show you how it's done. If she wants to play a card game, let her show you how it's done—even if you already know how to play. And acknowledge that you are impressed and proud of the child's mastery. She needs this kind of nurturing.

A hug or a kiss can go a long way toward bonding with your Low-Tolerant Child, or any child for that matter. And be attentive to those times when he needs to talk with you, or he may have to release pent-up feelings. Barring the not-infrequent times when he is emotionally invested in getting his own way, you should respond immediately to the genuine emotional needs of your child.

And finally, make time to sit with him and look over old family pictures. This is always extremely touching when I have families do it in my office. Children typically have many questions for their parents, and they often share memories with them. The goal here is not accuracy in recollection. It is a time to recall when things were simpler. It's a time to focus on how much you love each other as you look beyond the current struggles. And it is a time for your child to understand how valuable he is simply because of who he is. Such an activity brings children and parents closer and often breaks down the defensive armors that obstruct healing and moving ahead as a family team.

26

The Anxious/Insecure Child

Finally we come to the Anxious/Insecure Child. These are children who manipulate primarily out of a craving for love, attention, and nurturance. They are also prone to attempts at evening the score (which I will explain below). Parents of Anxious/Insecure Children are likely to face a complex pattern of vacillation between assertiveness and insecurity. This paradox is confusing to parents, who may be unsure if their children are really hurting emotionally or simply fabricating emotions to get needs met. Fortunately, there are many things that parents of an Anxious/Insecure Child can do to reduce his need to engage his Tools of Power.

Let's begin by describing the Anxious/Insecure Child through a list of common characteristics. Although this is a list of typical characteristics, your child may not exhibit all of them. Also, presentation varies wildly.

The Anxious/Insecure Child:

1. Often whines, pouts, or plays the victim.

2. Often worries or complains about bodily aches and pains.

3. Often lashes out when things don't go his way.

4. Possesses a heightened need to be loved and accepted by his parents or caregivers.

5. Cannot tolerate emotional distance from parents or caregivers.

6. May display social problems such as isolation, avoidance of peer interaction, shyness, or fear of rejection.

7. May be overly suspicious of others.

8. May be irritable.

9. May behave immaturely—often insisting on sleeping with parents, fearing the dark, and fearing being alone.

10. May be overly harsh on himself.

11. Often feigns weakness or frailty as a means of getting needs met.

12. Lacks confidence and self-esteem.

The Anxious/Insecure Child often plays the victim because he has learned early on that this is the most efficient way to arouse parental sympathies, and he is expert at tapping into the innate parental desire to protect and shield children from pain (situational happiness).

In my practice, I often work with parents who sleep in separate rooms because of a child's "need" to sleep with one of the parents. A child who sleeps with a parent as late as the age of ten (not as uncommon as it may sound) is anxious/insecure, and by allowing this behavior to persist, the parent is playing into that insecurity.

If a child perpetually complains of bodily aches and pains, or what we refer to as "somatic concerns," it is usually because he has difficulty getting his needs met verbally. Such a child holds on to anxiety and stress with no productive means of relieving it. This is also common to adults in cultures in which it is considered inappropriate to talk about personal problems. In such cultures, adults as well as children often exhibit psychosomatic behavior and express their worries and reach out for help through bodily complaints. This is what we see in the Anxious/Insecure Child.

The Anxious/Insecure Child is burdened with poor coping skills. Anything can become a crisis, and she is prone to lashing out when things do not go her way. And as any parent of an Anxious/Insecure Child will tell you, these children can become quite malicious. Because they feel pain, they lash out at others, often transferring the pain to them. But after acting out, and because they fear distancing themselves from parents or caregivers, they are typically profusely apologetic. Many parents are relieved by this and conclude that the child, after all, "has a conscience." I am skeptical of this conclusion. My sense is that the child is contrite only because she doesn't have the inner strength to cope with the discomfort and emotional distance caused by a conflict.

Fast-forward to the time your child begins to date and perhaps marry. Her relationships will be troubled because she is not capable of coping with the inevitable conflicts. She will think only of her own concerns and will consequently drive others away. Her potential partner will find her to be the controlling Anxious/Insecure Adult. I tell parents that though it may appear that their child has a conscience, when she is emotionally invested in a goal, she is really unable to consider the feelings of others—which is the root of conscience.

Such children (and adults—if such behavior is not treated) will do almost anything to be reaccepted by the person who has been subject to their attacks. Their need for acceptance is so great that many parents of Anxious/Insecure Children report that their child will not give them space after an argument. If they go to their bedroom to calm down, their child will bang at the door and cry in protest. As trying and as frustrating as this can be for the parent, the intensity of emotion is nearly unbearable for the child.

It is obvious why many of these children experience social problems. They can be controlling, self-centered, and prone to engaging in tactics designed to cause guilt in others, and as a result, they turn others away and avoid contact out of fear of being rejected. Some Anxious/Insecure Children that I see devalue their peers out of rejection aversion. Some of these children develop elaborate persecutory fantasies about what their peers say and do behind their backs. Consequently, it is challenging to attempt to place these children in situations where they can work on improving their social interactions. The very activities that could improve their social skills are activities that they dread and avoid. If they can learn the do's and don'ts of social behavior and forge friendships, they are capable of maturing fairly quickly. Like nearly everyone, they can learn to accept and be accepted by others.

With the fear and anxiety that these children carry within them, it is easy to see why the Anxious/Insecure Child has a tendency to be irritable. Like those who are depressed, these children often have negative thoughts about themselves and others, and these negative thoughts may be voiced. They do this to protect themselves from their fear of disappointment, failure, or rejection. Such a child tends to snap at others when things don't go her way. Parents are often left feeling that because of this irritability and tendency to complain, nothing they ever do for their child will be good enough. It is at these times that parents need to keep the I-WIN (I Want It Now) mentality in perspective. Of course what you do is good enough, but it only lasts so long. The Anxious/Insecure Child is a ravenous consumer of the energy of others. Her feelings of anxiety are often relieved only by instant gratification. Anything you do as a parent will suffice only for a short period of time. And when the gratification wears out, what you've done for her will most likely be forgotten or devalued as well.

As a parent, you shouldn't allow yourself to fall prey to feelings of being devalued by this process. Giving in to your child's situational anxiety is only placing a bandage on the bigger problem—the state of anxiety with which your child constantly struggles.

If you ever doubt the level of anxiety experienced by these children, you need only to listen to their language. They are unusually critical of themselves. Their utterances are laced with statements such as, "I can't do it," "It's too hard," or "I'm afraid," and self-deprecating comments such as, "I'm ugly," "I'm stupid," or "Nobody likes me." This verbally expressed low level of self-esteem is backed up by behavior. The Anxious/Insecure Child gives up easily or avoids even trying out of fear of failure. Parents aren't sure how to respond. If I push her too hard, might her fear of failure come true? And would I be guilty of setting her up for failure?

The Anxious/Insecure Child often displays immature behavior. She may be inordinately afraid of the dark and insist on sleeping with a parent, and she typically protests and has meltdowns when the parent refuses to meet her demands. These meltdowns likely leave parents feeling that if they insist on age-appropriate behavior, they may cause more harm than by allowing the child to act immaturely. It is this concern that often brings these families to my office.

It is critical in such dynamics that parents learn ways to help their children strengthen their coping skills. The Anxious/Insecure Child actually feels a sense of pride when she accomplishes a goal, such as learning to sleep in her own bed. It may not be apparent, but when these children feel a need to sleep in their parents' bed, they are typically embarrassed and shamed.

That's right, I said "shamed." After all, what ten-year-old would feel proud of her fear of sleeping alone? For that matter, what thirteen-year-old would feel anything but shame about her fear of staying home alone? Or that she is afraid to go to camp with her classmates? Or worse, to admit that she has no friends? This shame accompanies the child most of her waking hours and, with it, the concomitant low self-esteem. Self-esteem comes with mastery, and the Anxious/Insecure Child has few occasions to feel masterful.

Because she avoids situations that might subject her to failure, she never becomes master of her fate or, in her view, master of anything at all. By avoiding risks, she never makes the necessary move from mastery to self-esteem. But this is a self-defeating trap from which you can help her break free.

[PROACTIVE MEASURES]

You, the parent—the most important person in your child's life and the one whom he looks up to—can both guide and encourage your child to take steps toward mastering first the little things, then moving on toward greater goals. Here are some tips for doing this:

1. Keep your own emotional reactions to a minimum when at all possible.

2. Teach your child how to use language appropriately to get his needs met.

3. Limit your behavioral goals to just one or two at a time.

4. Seek out activities in which your child has a good chance of experiencing a sense of mastery.

5. Have your child track his levels of anxiety.

6. Facilitate and supervise one-on-one social interactions.

7. Help your child interpret social interactions accurately (steer him away from self-deprecating or distorted interpretations).

The starting point in working with the Anxious/Insecure Child is to maintain your integrity and composure. Be aware that he is prone to feelings of rejection and that whenever you raise your voice in anger over something he has done wrong, he might feel rejected and distanced from you. On the other hand, if you keep cool and deliver a fair and logical consequence for an inappropriate behavior, your child might recoil at the punishment, but he is less likely to internalize it. Remember that he has a heightened sensitivity to any expression of disapproval coming from you.

Many parents in my private practice have seen stress levels in the home decrease as they heeded this advice. These parents learned to deliver consequences that were fair and consistent. And they did it without raising their voices. Although the Anxious/Insecure Child has trouble accepting rejection, he *can* accept consequences. After all, these kids are typically harder on themselves than anyone else could ever be. Often, suffering a consequence can allow them to feel closer to a parent because they feel that they have paid their debt for an inappropriate behavior. This, in turn, allows them to move on. Remember, have the integrity to stay calm in the presence of your Anxious/Insecure Child. Doing so will limit the frustration you will suffer as a parent.

One of the biggest impairments I have observed in the Anxious/Insecure Child is his inability to verbalize his feelings. This is likely because he has learned to get what he needs through emotional appeals, often by playing the victim. But children who are insecure also fear that others will discount what they have to say. Signals of this fear are phrases like, "You never listen to anything I say." This has to be turned around. He needs to be taught how to be assertive and how to make his words count.

Say "use your words" when your child is responding emotionally, and reward him when he does so. Rewarding a child doesn't mean always giving him his way, but consider repeating back to him what you have heard him say, and if he articulates his needs well, think twice about rejecting his request. It's a matter of rewarding good behavior.

When I was training to become a psychologist, I had a client in group therapy whose name was Bruce. Fifty-six years old and suffering from bad arthritis, he hated taking what we called "nature walks." But no one knew about Bruce's discomfort because he never expressed his feelings. After about a year of counseling, Bruce finally asserted himself in the group. During one of our stress-management sessions, we suggested taking a walk, and suddenly Bruce yelled out, "I don't want to take a fucking walk!" Startled and stunned, the group laughed along with Bruce, who went on to explain that the walks brought him nothing but pain from his bad hips. It was the first time we had been made aware of this, and it was a breakthrough for Bruce. We didn't take the walk, but we all got to know one another a little better in that session. I tell you this story to illustrate how hard it can be for some individuals—even adults—to learn how to *use their words* to get what they want. Bruce was well into middle age, yet it took him a year to mutter his crudely stated objections. Over time, his ability to express himself became more refined. Your child might progress even more slowly than Bruce, and you will therefore have to have realistic expectations for his behavior. Be patient, and you will be rewarded. Your child's first attempt at using his words might be crude and unrefined. That's okay. Stick with it and praise him for his efforts. He will mature.

The same principles apply to helping your child improve inappropriate behaviors. You never want to work on more than one or two behaviors at a time. I often have parents make a list of the behaviors in their children that they would like to see change. I tell parents that making this list will allow them to feel more confident that they will eventually get to all the behaviors they want to see change. But any child would be overwhelmed by such a list and would take it as the harshest of criticisms.

You might also focus on what I call "the behavior of the day." But that, too, can be threatening for your child, and it rarely brings about change. It is best to keep in mind the changes you would like to facilitate, and reward your child with verbal praise when he has mastered a behavior you have targeted. Then move on to another goal. Your child will appreciate the opportunity to "graduate" from one behavior to another.

One way to work on behaviors is to develop an inconspicuous password. If the behavior you are working on is your child's ability to use his words when he is upset or sad, you may choose a password like "Leno." The password should be meaningful to the child. It helps when the child can give you the password and the reason he chose it. In this case, the child may have chosen the word "Leno" because he thought about Jay Leno's use of words throughout his five-minute monologue. A password should never be known to your child's peers. The point is that you should be able to use it in public without calling attention to your child. For example, you may witness the onset of a tantrum while your child is playing with a peer. Rather than saying, "Don't throw a tantrum. Use your words to express your feelings," you could simply say "Jay Leno's on tonight." This password will allow you to prompt your child without risk of embarrassing him in front of his friend.

No matter how you work on the behavior, be sure to set realistic expectations and have patience for the time it will take your child to grow. Simply pointing out why a behavior is inappropriate to your child is not enough. You are asking the Anxious/Insecure Child to change much more than a behavior. For him, it is an ingrained way of coping and dealing with the world.

In children, self-confidence comes in part by gaining a sense of mastery. As a parent, your job entails seeking out those activities that will allow your child to experience that sense of mastery. This is particularly important for the Anxious/Insecure Child. As the saying goes, accentuate the positive. To do this, you must pay attention to your child's strengths and weaknesses. If your child finds it hard to participate in sports, don't push him to play. No sense of mastery will ever come from being chosen last or sitting on the bench during every game. Parents who push their children into situations like this are often living vicariously through their children and not letting them find their own means of expression. The boy who doesn't like soccer may be interested in the violin. Sign him up for violin lessons and encourage him to join a school orchestra. Sports are not the only social activities out there. Facilitating his mastery of something he really loves will go a long way toward building self-esteem. But there is another important aspect of self-esteem.

Many parents of the Anxious/Insecure Child are anxious adults. And as we know, anxious people tend to focus on problems rather than successes. As a parent, you need to understand that your child internalizes the messages, both verbal and nonverbal, that you convey. This is normal. He can flourish in a piano recital, but you can take away his sense of mastery with a badly timed critical statement. You need to get in the habit of noticing successes and pointing them out. Telling your child how proud you are of him for taking a risk can be even more rewarding than winning a contest. The Anxious/Insecure Child wants to please his parents and make them proud. When the parent he idealizes is proud of him, it makes it that much easier for him to be proud of himself. Notice the good in your child; he won't likely notice it in himself.

Apart from lacking confidence in themselves, Anxious/Insecure Children are also wary about coping with their anxiety, so that it inevitably mushrooms into something greater than the sum of its parts. For this reason, parents must help their children understand that anxiety is only temporary and that they are equipped to deal with it. One way to do this is to teach your child to measure her anxiety. The following is a method I use with my patients.

I describe anxiety relative to its intensity on a scale from zero to ten, with ten representing the greatest intensity. I tell families that only when the child's anxiety is so great that it feels like it is unbearable does it rate a ten. Between those two extremes is the score of five, representing moderate anxiety. After the scale is understood by all, I then tell the child to measure her anxiety when prompted by a parent. Scores are to be charted every minute until the point at which the score of zero is recorded for two consecutive minutes. Parents are instructed to prompt their child to measure their anxiety when they feel that the child is struggling to contain it. This scoring system is never used out of frustration on the part of the parents; it is used only as a tool to help the Anxious/Insecure Child. It will allow the child to gauge how long the anxiety will last in addition to educating the child on the fact that the anxiety is only temporary. These are both important elements necessary for the nurturing of coping skills in the Anxious/Insecure Child. It also turns the precipitating action into a kind of a game, which can quickly diffuse anxiety.

Finally, there is the problem of social interaction. Anxious children invariably suffer from social problems that may present themselves in a number of different ways. Perhaps your child avoids peer contact or is controlling in her relationships with peers. Perhaps she has little patience with their shortcomings, or maybe she resists sharing friends with others. Whatever the case, she needs your help to improve peer relationships.

One of the more effective ways of helping your child in this area is to provide opportunities for peer interaction and coach her when she is involved with her peers. As mentioned above, it is important to sit down with your child before any interaction and point out things you would like to work on, assigning a password that will allow your child to be prompted without embarrassment. Research suggests that children are most likely to learn how to improve social skills through practice—that is, while they are in the midst of actual encounters with others.

To make all this work to his or her benefit, it is important for you to get to know your child's friends as well as their parents. You need to know which children are "safe" and which your child should avoid. A safe peer is one who will not turn on your child and one you can count on to be consistently cordial. You want your child to be able to make mistakes without fearing harsh criticism or rejection. Knowing other parents is essential to providing a safe environment for your child to experiment and grow socially.

Taking all these measures into account, remember the rule of thumb that *you never want to work on too many behaviors at a time*. If your child tends to talk over the utterances of others and always wants to choose activities, stick to correcting the talking over others until that is ameliorated. It is not possible for your child to benefit from these exercises if you focus on too many behaviors at once. She will only feel excessively criticized, and you will feel frustrated. Be patient but remain focused.

A classic reaction in your child as she engages in peer interactions may be that she tends to exaggerate the statements or behavior of others. She may feel that a peer no longer likes her because the peer went off to eat lunch with someone else one day at school. Or she may deduce that her friend no longer likes her because she hurt his feelings when they were walking home from school. These are both examples of the distorted perceptions of the Anxious/Insecure Child, and they most often derive from a *heightened sensitivity to rejection*. You must be aware of these fears and help your child find the true reason for a friend's behavior. For example, you might have to explain, in as sensitive a way as you can, that friends can want to spend some time alone with other friends or that fights come up even between the best of friends, but that the friendships can still endure if they are solid enough.

Your child also needs to understand how to communicate her feelings to a friend in uncomfortable situations. The Anxious/Insecure Child has a way of interpreting the actions of her peers in a very self-critical way. And your job as a parent is to help her understand other, less critical reasons behind the actions of others. If you don't help your child in this area, you may find that she will avoid peer contact or simply write off certain friends. These are very unhealthy traits for a child to learn.

Helping your Anxious/Insecure Child is a multifaceted process. Making the changes I have suggested above should lessen your child's need to rely on her Tools of Power to get what she wants or needs. But keep in mind that no matter what countermeasures and strategies you use, they won't work unless you stay calm and maintain your integrity as a parent.

Final Note

While I was writing this book, the media were full of stories about the latest lurid exploits of socialites and celebrities of the day. Many of these stories seem like the tragic results of the seventeen Tools of Power run amok. Because apparently no one cared enough about these young adults, some of whose screen careers plummeted as their antisocial behavior spread across newsstands and the Internet, their forays into adulthood have been disastrous. In some cases, the legal system has become the surrogate parent, with judges replacing parents who could never say no.

The truth is that children who use their Tools of Power in an attempt to get what they want are really crying out for you, the parent, to take control—to guide them. You are their protector. Following the suggestions in this book should help you with your goals of guiding your child safely through the many pitfalls of adolescence into safe and successful adulthood.

Children are looking for guidance and protection, despite their protestations to the contrary. You owe it to them and to yourself to give it to them. By understanding the Tools of Power and how your child employs them, and by following the countermeasures I've spelled out, you can take control and become a more successful parent.

Now that you know how the tools work, you are also more aware of how to meet your child's interpersonal needs so that you can reduce his or her manipulative behaviors in the future.

You are not alone in your struggle as a parent. Parenting is one of the toughest jobs anyone can have, and it is a challenge for which few of us are well prepared. Perhaps this advice can help light the way.

Five Steps for Imposing a Restriction

1. **Determine a privilege (something your child loves to do) to be regulated.** The privilege needs to be *something you can control.* Television is not controllable, because when you leave home, your child can turn it on. A video game console or a computer is controllable because you can easily remove the controller or keyboard and take it with you when you leave home.

2. **Determine a time frame that this privilege will be available.** It is best to place the privilege *at the end of the day* to maximize the leverage you achieve by regulating it. If you place it at the beginning of the day, your child can take advantage of the privilege early and has no need to comply with your directives for the rest of the day.

3. **Determine the length of time that the privilege will be granted.** For example, if you decide that your child should be allowed to play video games only ninety minutes a day, you can tell your child, "Video games are only going to be played in our home between seven and eight thirty in the evening."

4. **Determine the length of time that you will "chip away" from the privilege as a consequence.** If you normally allow sixty minutes of video game use, a reasonable consequence would be to take away ten minutes. Or you might double the amount of time the child has demonstrated undesirable behavior ("For every minute you continue to act this way, you will lose two minutes of your video game time").

5. **Have a meeting with your child.** Let her know that you will help her improve on a particular goal. For example, the goal may be following directions before you count to three (giving ten seconds between each count). Inform your child that if she fails to respond to your directive and you count to three, then she will lose ten minutes of her video game time. If her privilege usually begins at 7:00 p.m., getting to three would result in it beginning at 7:10 p.m. The end time should always remain the same.

Remember to start the time restriction from the beginning of the regulated time block. This is the best way to maximize your leverage.

Special Acknowledgement

I wish to extend a special thank-you to Michael Moreau, my personal editor, who helped me get my thoughts and ideas in order. Michael Moreau has been a writer and editor for more than twenty years. He has been published in the *Los Angeles Times* and various magazines, including *Westways, Crisis, California Lawyer,* and *Surfer.* His book, *John Fante and H. L. Mencken: A Personal Correspondence,* was published in 1989 by Black Sparrow Press. He currently chairs the Journalism Department at Glendale Community College in Glendale, California.

Index

218 Index

Diagnostic and Statistical Manual-IV-TR (DSM-IV-ITR)
  attention-deficit/hyperactivity disorder in, 158
  Oppositional Defiant Disorder in, 167–68
Difference of opinion, between parents, 84–85
Disappointment
  with Casting Doubt, 122
  with Covert Operations, 78
  of Low-Tolerant Child, 180–82
  lying with, 78
  with Steamrolling, 71
Discussion
  of decisions, 94–95
  with Irrational Logic, 50–51
  personal, 192
Disneyland Parent, 109
Disrespect, 75
Divide and Conquer
  anger with, 82–83
  consequences with, 86–87
  countermeasures for, 85–87
  Principle of Restoration with, 86–87
  scenario of, 83–84
Divorce
  anxiety about, 101–2
  boundaries after, 105–6, 108, 110–11
  with Confrontation and Protest, 58
  with Forging the Friendship, 105–6, 108, 110–11
  with Shutting Down, 40

Embarrassment, 130
Emotional Blackmail, 25–26
  consistency with, 31
  countermeasures for, 30–31
  emotions with, 30
  scenarios of, 23–24, 28
Emotional buttons, 6, 13–14
  anger as, 5
  with Covert Operations, 79–80
  with Oppositional Child, 168–69
  sadness as, 4
  score-evening with, 141
Emotional distance
  with Anxious/Insecure Child, 196
  with Confrontation and Protest, 61–62
  in parenting, 61–62

Emotional investment
  with Irrational Logic, 51
  with Playing the Victim, 102–3
  with Tactical Engagement, 95
Emotions, of children
  of Anxious/Insecure Child, 202, 203
  as behavioral cause, 12–13
  with Emotional Blackmail, 30
  fickleness of, 23
  of Low-Tolerant Child, 194
  with Playing the Victim, 102–4
  responsibility for, 30
  separation of, 102–4
  verbalizing of, 202, 203
Emotions, of parents
  with Forging the Friendship, 106, 108, 110
  neediness with, 106, 108, 110
  with Punishment, 38–39
Empathy
  of child, 15–17
  of parents, 103
Empowerment
  of Low-Tolerant Child, 191
  from manipulation, 139–40
Entitlement
  of Impulsive Child, 164
  of Low-Tolerant Child, 180–81
  with Punishment, 35–36
Exaggeration, 207–8
Expectation
  for Impulsive Child, 164, 166
  for Low-Tolerant Child, 180–81

Failure
  fear of, 199–200
  at school, 118
Family, 186
Fear, 137
  with Anxious/Insecure Child, 199–200
  of consequences, 12
  of failure, 199–200
Fidgeting, 159
Forgetfulness, 159
Forging the Friendship
  advice with, 109
  bed-sharing with, 106, 109
  consequences with, 109
  countermeasures for, 110–11
  divorce with, 105–6, 108, 110–11
  parents' emotions with, 106, 108, 110

About the Author

Photo by Julie West Photography

Dr. David Swanson is a psychologist practicing in Encino, California. He holds two master's degrees and a doctoral degree in the field of clinical psychology. Dr. Swanson is well known for his work with children, teens, families, and parents. In addition to his practice, Dr. Swanson is frequently called upon as an expert for several television outlets. He has appeared on NBC, CBS, *Extra*, and *The Early Show*. He has consulted for several local and national radio stations, including CNN and ABC Talk Radio. A married father of three, Dr. Swanson strives to help families and children live happier, healthier lives.

To learn more about Dr. Swanson, visit www.DrDavidSwanson .com. To view and subscribe to Dr. Swanson's free online quarterly newsletter containing video blogs from Dr. Swanson, visit www.TheHealthyChild.info.